ROBERTO MANCINI

First published by Carlton Books Ltd in 2012

Carlton Books Ltd
20 Mortimer Street
London W1T 3JW

A CIP catalogue record for this book is available from the British Library.

ISBN: 978-0-23300-368-9

Printed and bound by CPI Group (UK) Ltd, Croydon, CR0 4YY

ROBERTO MANCINI

The man behind Manchester City's greatest-ever season

STUART BRENNAN

ANDRE
DEUTSCH

Contents

Introduction

When Sir Alex Ferguson celebrated the 25th anniversary of his Manchester United reign, it was pointed out that Manchester City had got through 14 managers in that same period. The Scot's reply was instantaneous: "I wish it was 15," he said with a rueful smile. Eleven days earlier, he had seen "number 15", Roberto Mancini, guide his side to a 6–1 win at Old Trafford, which shocked the football world. It was not just that result, the worst day of Ferguson's football life, which prompted the United manager's comment. He knew that in the complex, driven, debonair Italian he had found a worthy adversary, someone capable not just of matching his team's Manchester supremacy, but also of overhauling them as the major power in English football. He was right to be concerned.

Mancini had been a surprise selection as the new City manager when the oil-rich owners of the club decided, in the winter of 2009, that Mark Hughes was not the man they needed to take the club forward. The Italian had been a brilliant, sometimes breathtaking, player, who had courted controversy and built himself a power base at Sampdoria which far exceeded that of a normal footballer. He would sit in board meetings, influence team selection, and help to design the new kit – "he would have driven the team bus if we had let him," said his old manager and mentor Sven-Goran Eriksson.

As a coach and manager himself, Mancini was baptized in the fires
which threatened to engulf Italian football entirely in the opening
decade of the 21st century. The money pouring into the game
through new television and commercial deals meant that football –
always an important part of Italian life – was suddenly big business.
This meant that to rely on winning fairly was too much of a risk, so
cheating became an industry in itself. Alongside the match-fixing,
the fan violence at games was getting out of hand, and several clubs
were financially imploding.

It was little wonder that Mancini, who had spent most of his
playing career suspecting that he was being cheated, should decide
he'd had his fill of the football storm in his homeland and, having
proved himself with a hat-trick of Serie A titles with Internazionale,
head for the relatively calm waters of the English Premier League.

When he is asked questions about the pressure of being the
manager of Manchester City, whose owners have mapped out a
progressive route to the top of European football, he refuses to
accept that there is any pressure. He remembers the days when Lazio
fans were climbing the fences of the training ground after a derby
defeat, with trouble in mind. He thinks of his players at Fiorentina,
angry and threatening to sue after six months without pay. And he
considers the pressure to succeed which led to the men he worked
for, at Fiorentina and Lazio, spending time behind bars.

Little wonder that the image he presents to the media is of
the cool, collected, suave Italian, immaculately tailored,
occasionally running his hands through his flowing locks, his face
always ready to crease into a laugh. City fans, many of whom
worried at first that the club owners had brought in a man with
no Premier League experience, and limited credentials in Italy,

soon warmed to him, and made him one of their own, even re-christening him "Bobby Manc".

Those who work with him, and for him, paint a different picture. His temper is legendary, and his desire for victory insatiable. That drive can bring him into conflict with players, club officials, referees, opposing managers – anyone he perceives to be hindering the cause. But it also brings results and, if you get on board and match his single-mindedness, it brings the very best of rewards.

Mancini has ruffled a few feathers at City, and some found his personality hard to take at first – to some he appeared cold and aloof to the point of arrogance. As he has settled into the job, he has permitted glimpses into the depths of his personality, with its contradictions – a shy man who has a powerful belief in his own ability, a deeply religious individual who refuses to turn the other cheek, a multi-millionaire who cycles to work every morning. In an interview with the Italian newspaper *La Repubblica* in 1988 Mancini suggested he might be misunderstood: "I am outspoken but I am also an introvert, so maybe that sometimes comes across as obnoxious," he said. "But if someone shows himself to be my friend, I would give them anything, even more …"

He was perhaps at his happiest at that time, when he was a player at Sampdoria, the unfashionable Genoese club which he helped to transform into national champions, whose team played with a swagger and style unusual in Italy. He and fellow striker Gianluca Vialli were afforded god-like status by the fans, and the team was bonded by a pact that they would remain together until they had won the title. That piece of Sampdoria spirit is now working its magic at City, with Mancini bringing old team-mates Attilio Lombardo and Fausto Salsano to help him, while David Platt – who joined Samp after their Scudetto year – is another prop for the manager. By studying Mancini's story – his battles with officialdom, the suspicion about referees, the tempestuous behaviour of his youth, and his regrets over his under-achieving international career – you can begin to understand his approach to the handling of difficult superstars like Carlos Tevez and Mario Balotelli, and why he sometimes suspects that some of the established elite clubs in England have undue influence.

His often infuriating refusal to acknowledge the abilities of some of his players, especially young ones, is perhaps rooted in the way his own father would be his biggest critic, driving the young Roberto towards unattainable perfection. When Sergio Aguero, making his first start at the Etihad Stadium, scored a hat-trick of high quality, his team-mates signed the match ball as a memento, adding their own congratulations. Mancini's scribbled message was "not bad".

The infamous dugout row with Carlos Tevez at Bayern Munich in 2011 was also not a new thing for Mancini. He had similar disagreements with Marco Materazzi and Luis Figo during his days as Inter coach. That is one of many themes which recur throughout his career.

Perhaps the most significant of those themes is his love of being the underdog, of bringing success where there was none. He did that spectacularly at Sampdoria, when instead he could easily have fallen for the charms of AC Milan or Juventus, who would have snapped him up without blinking. His brief dalliance as a player in England, at the end of his career, was not at a glamour club suited to his talents, but at modest Leicester City. Their manager Peter Taylor recalled the day he started training: "The lads stood there open-mouthed when Roberto started bending free-kicks in from all over the place. They quickly started calling him 'The Legend'."

As a manager and coach, he walked into a financial blizzard at Fiorentina and helped them win the Coppa Italia, and he led Inter out of a trophy-less wilderness before being sacked for his troubles. Then it was on to City, whose fans were screaming out for success and, like Inter, were forced to watch their neighbours garner glory year after year, making their own failings more stark.

The prospect of taking on Ferguson, the Godfather of Premier League managers and untouchable lord of all he surveys at Manchester United, did not faze Mancini at all. He has always shown due respect to his cross-town rival, without deference. The moment when they went eyeball to eyeball in the technical area during the crucial Manchester derby of April 2012, as City wrestled control of the Premier League trophy back out of United's hands, was symbolic. Ferguson can be a bully, but he was not having his own way with Mancini, much to the delight of the City fans. It was perhaps the moment when the older man finally realized there was a younger gun in town now, and he wasn't going away any time soon.

Perhaps, then, the most fitting tribute of all to Mancini's management style was the one paid by Ferguson in the match programme for the derby match earlier in the 2011–12 season, when the feud between the City boss and Tevez, who had joined the Blues from United, was at its height.

"If anyone ever doubted the ability of Mancini as a manager you just have to study his handling of the Carlos Tevez situation recently, for this was a masterclass in management," wrote Ferguson. "When Carlos appeared reluctant to come on as a substitute, I saw a coach angry and disturbed – and rightly so because nobody should be bigger at a club than the manager. He is the man who must have absolute authority, and to give way to a challenge to his control is the biggest mistake a boss can make. I am not saying this to have a go at Carlos.

"There will be cynics who will say I have it in for him because of the circumstances through which he left Old Trafford under something of a cloud. But I never had a problem with Carlos, and I am only speaking critically of him now because of my understanding of the difficult job all managers face. Carlos no doubt felt aggrieved, and I am sure he still does, but there are important principles at play here and there has to be a limit to what a head coach can tolerate. If there is a clear attempt to defy the authority of the manager, then he has to react – and vigorously so.

"Management these days has become much more complicated, not least because of the enormous amounts of money players can earn, and you cannot afford to pander to that kind of power. The City boss's reaction was spot-on and sent a clear message to the rest of the players, not just at Eastlands but also throughout the game. His handling of the situation distinguished him in managerial terms. I always admire the courage to do right and that was what we are seeing here."

* A note on the words "coach" and "manager". In Italy, the English management role is split between the coach, who looks after the team on a day-to-day basis, and the sporting director, who handles transfer negotiations and contracts. In England, those two roles are traditionally performed by the same man, the manager. In England, writers refer to Italian coaches as "managers". I refrained from doing that, simply because Mancini broke that particular mould in Serie A by combining both roles as he tried to prevent a financial meltdown at Fiorentina. Whereas at Lazio and Inter he was a coach, at Fiorentina he was an English-style manager.

Chapter One
A Blue Moon Rising

For five frantic, feverish minutes, Roberto Mancini added another vowel to his nickname. The man tagged "Bobby Manc" by the adoring Manchester City fans transformed, before 47,435 pairs of eyes, into Bobby Manic. He squatted and snarled, gesticulated and swore in Italian, barely able to contain his vein-bulging fury at what was happening before him.

It was understandable. As the final match of the 2011–12 season moved into added time, it was as if Mancini's whole life had been heading for this point. He had been a huge success in Italy, as player and manager, but this was a bigger challenge, to change the fate of one of football's down-trodden underdogs, and win the biggest prize in an alien football culture.

Mancini is said by Italian football people to be *baciato dalla grazia*, or "kissed by good fortune". A few more hangdog City fans wryly commented that he might need more than good fortune, and a few bob to spend, if he was to break the curse which seemed to afflict City. This wasn't Manchester City. "Typical City" was the club which Mancini had agreed to lead. It was a tag which summed up the club's amazing capacity for turning glory into farce, and to let their supporters down just when they were beginning to believe. This was the club which, in 1927, had lost out to Portsmouth on promotion

1

by 0.0041 of a goal, in the complex days when goal average, rather than goal difference, decided league places. And that was after they won 8–0 on the final day of the season. The year before, they had been relegated after scoring an incredible 89 goals – more than any other relegated team in history. In 1962, they led Luton 6–2 in an FA Cup tie, with Denis Law having scored all six, when the game was abandoned due to a waterlogged pitch. Naturally, City lost the replay, 3–1.

Former chairman Francis Lee, who had been a goalscoring hero in the last City team to win the league, in 1968, had summed it all up memorably: "If cups were awarded for cock-ups, you would not be able to move in Manchester City's boardroom."

What made it worse was that while City had slid through 30 years of disaster and despair, neighbours United were enjoying the most successful spell of any club in English football history. Their manager Sir Alex Ferguson derisively referred to City's stadium as the "Temple of Doom", and even City fan and BBC radio wordsmith Stuart Hall affectionately called it the "Theatre of Base Comedy", by way of contrast to United's snooty labelling of their Old Trafford home as the "Theatre of Dreams".

As the last game of the 2011–12 season entered those fateful five minutes at the Etihad Stadium, Typical City looked to be playing its greatest trick of all, painful in its cruelty. Certainly no-one was laughing at the Theatre of Base Comedy. This was not even remotely funny to the City fans who had gathered to witness the day when they ceased to be Typical City forever, and ushered in a glorious new era in their chequered history.

With the Blues needing three points to end a 44-year wait for a league title, it had all looked simple for them as they faced Queen's

Park Rangers, the worst travellers in the Premier League. City had an almost perfect home record, having won 17 and drawn one, and after disposing of rivals Manchester United and then being impressively solid in victory in a tough match at Newcastle, it seemed a formality that QPR would be brushed aside as the Blues completed the job.

City stood level on points with United, but with a goal difference superior by eight, so victory would ensure the title barring a freakishly one-sided win for the Reds at Sunderland. It looked like a cinch. But, as Mancini says with a frequency that makes for banality, "This is football."

Now it had gone horribly wrong. QPR had not only come from behind, they had survived the dismissal of their perennial bad boy and former City star Joey Barton, to take the lead and stun the Etihad Stadium into silence. With United leading through a Wayne Rooney goal, it seemed like the demons which had haunted City for 44 years were once again spreading their wings above east Manchester, plunging the City fans beneath into despair.

Those supporters were looking at each other, but not in disbelief, because they have become used to disappointment and despair down the years. The looks were more about resignation, a crushing resignation to the belief that the phrase "Typical City" had survived the expensive new broom which the oil-rich owners had been applying to every corner of the club since their 2008 takeover. One fan, sitting in front of the press box, turned to the journalists and said, in a voice heaving with hurt: "Why do they do it to us, every time?"

There were also serious question marks hanging over Mancini's future. It would seem crazy in any other industry, but the difference between success and failure for a football manager can be as narrow as a goalpost. The ball goes one side, and you are a hero. It goes the other side, and you get the sack, and a "failure" stamp on your CV.

There was plenty of speculation that Mancini might be moved on if his team finished the season trophy-less. The owners had made soothing noises, and Mancini's relationship with Sheikh Mansour, and particularly with the hands-on chairman Khaldoon Al Mubarak, has always been a strong one. But the Abu Dhabi royal family are not used to failure.

If Mancini's team were to lose the title on the final day, when they virtually had it in the bag, it would raise all sorts of negative questions. How had they lost their way when they were cutting such a swathe through the league in the autumn, and with so many players available? Had Mancini's handling of the renegade Carlos Tevez and his kid-glove treatment of the maverick striker Mario Balotelli cost them the title? And how could they blow it when all they had to do was see off a QPR team which had been lying down for the opposition in the closing months of the season? But just as the negatives are multiplied when things go wrong, the positives are enhanced when they go right – and so it was to prove.

The 47,000-plus in the stadium, and the millions watching worldwide, had it wrong. City weren't finished. And they weren't finished because Mancini had instilled a new mentality into those players who were labouring on the pitch, staring ignominy in the face. He had maintained from day one in the job that his biggest challenge was not winning a trophy after 34 barren years, nor securing qualification for the Champions League. His toughest task was to rid the club, specifically the playing side, of the infection which meant they were forever doomed to play second fiddle, especially to United.

In the years since the League Cup triumph of 1976, City fans had come to wear their support for perennial losers as a badge of honour. Despite the defeats and the disasters, they were still there, proud of their club, fervent in their support. That was never going to be good enough for Mancini. He had to make those supporters believe, and to do that he had to make his players believe. And on May 13, 2011, with QPR leading 2–1 and the title hopes sliding into the abyss of broken dreams, it seemed that he had failed.

Some supporters had already left the stadium, not out of disloyalty, but simply finding the whole thing too painful. More misery, more let-down, more Red mockery.

But the one thing that could not be discerned was the mind-set of those 11 players in sky blue. Their crosses were being over-hit, their shots miscued, and ten-man QPR were defending with heart and nous. After the game, the City players were unanimous in saying that at no point did they doubt that they would come back and win the game. Apart from one or two fans who belong to that endangered species – the ultra-optimistic Manchester City fan – there were few others inside the stadium who felt the same way.

Mancini himself didn't have time to consider whether it was slipping away or not. He knew his team had been the best in the Premier League all season. They had scored more goals, and conceded fewer, than anyone in the top four divisions of English football. They had smashed six past United at Old Trafford, blitzed Tottenham for five at White Hart Lane, scored another six at Norwich, and some of their football had been breathtaking. But the winter winds had blown with chill reality, the runaway City express had slowed, and ugly doubts about whether they could tough it out and earn points when their form dipped, began to raise their heads.

Mancini had played a couple of jokers, bringing back Carlos Tevez in a pragmatic move which initially brought him much derision, and then relieving his players of the burden of title hopes by declaring that the race was finished. His repetition of that statement, after each City win and each United slip, became a standing, secret joke between Mancini and the nation. We knew he didn't mean it; he knew he didn't mean it; his players knew he didn't mean it, and United certainly knew he certainly didn't mean it. But it seemed to have done the trick, so he just kept on saying it. Such stuff is invested with the heady tag of "mind games" when in truth it was little more than a superstition, and a gentle jab at those sections of the media who had dismissed City's chances.

The Blues, seemingly down and out, had rallied with five straight wins as United stumbled, but now, with time dashing away, on the ultimate point of the sharp end of the season, those doubts about the Blues' mentality had revisited, and they were tenfold. Mancini had played the last two cards in his hand, putting on strikers Edin Dzeko, who had flattered to deceive all season, and Mario Balotelli, who had veered wildly between brilliance and buffoonery.

The manager's turmoil was there for everyone to see. A perfectionist as a player, he was helpless as his charges began making errors, rushing their work and showing signs of desperation and panic.

Then everything changed, and City were camped in the Rangers' half. Even so, on the couple of occasions they had fashioned clear goal chances, they had found the visitors' goalkeeper Paddy Kenny on inspired form. They were winning corners, but QPR centre backs

Anton Ferdinand – whose big brother Rio was playing for United that same day – and Clint Hill were keeping them out.

The fourth official's board showed that referee Mike Dean had signalled for five minutes of added time, but there were already 75 seconds of that played, and the score remained Manchester City 1, Queen's Park Rangers 2. Then the Blues had a corner, and David Silva, the little Spaniard who had been voted the club's player of the year by his fellow players, hastened across to take it. Goalkeeper Joe Hart began to make his way forward, desperate to add his height and strength in an attacking capacity, but was waved back.

He wasn't needed. The ball swung in and Dzeko, who had been derided at times for his lack of aerial power, given his 6ft 3in frame, rose to power home the header. Hope was instantly reborn. Perhaps City could grab another. Maybe Sunderland could sneak a late equalizer in the north-east.

Mancini allowed himself the most meagre celebration and was then back organizing his team for one final push. Thoroughness is Mancini's by-word, and this was no time to be complacent, even if QPR looked like a team that had given up any thoughts of scoring goals, especially as the message had gone out from their bench that relegation rivals Bolton had drawn at Stoke, and the London club were safe.

But QPR attacked, and there was now less than a minute left. Nigel de Jong, a first-half substitute for the influential Yaya Touré, carried the ball forward and played it to Sergio Aguero. The stocky little Argentine striker turned and played the ball in to Balotelli, who fell under challenge from Ferdinand but managed to stab it back into the path of Aguero. The striker, whose club record £38 million purchase had been urged by Mancini the previous summer, still had left back Taye Taiwo between him and the goal, but a deft touch to one side and a burst of speed took him into space.

Now it was just Kenny between him and everlasting Mancunian glory. But Aguero had been misfiring all game, and had already missed one glorious chance. It felt like someone had hit the "pause" button as for one moment the Premier League title, and perhaps the balance of power in Manchester football, in English football, was in the balance. Then Aguero cocked back that expensive right foot and thumped his shot unerringly between the QPR keeper and his near post.

The Etihad erupted in a frenzy of blue, a shower of joyous tears fell, and the pent-up emotion of so many years of being taunted and derided by the Reds, of being the down-at-heel neighbours to English football's biggest success story, was released in an electric surge which swept around the ground. The City bench cascaded down onto pitchside – substitutes, coaches, support staff, physios, interpreter and kit man flooding the technical area in unrestrained ecstasy.

Mancini had been standing, his hands in his jacket pockets, his neck craning forward to be closer to the action, as the last, fateful attack developed. When Aguero scored, he leapt into the arms of his assistant Brian Kidd and then allowed himself a fist-pumping victory jog onto the pitch. But while everyone else carried on with their wild celebration, Mancini was soon composed, and back barking out instructions, furiously tongue-lashing his team back into shape. Even with only seconds left on the clock, he was taking no chances, shouting instructions to his defence as they made their way back from the human pyramid they had formed on top of the prostrate Aguero.

But Rangers were spent, and the title – incredibly, startlingly, dramatically – belonged to the Blues.

Dean blew the whistle, and the celebrations were renewed as Mancini and Kidd embraced, the fitting combination of the Italian maestro and the working-class Mancunian lad born just a few hundred yards from the scenes of triumph. One of Mancini's Italian support staff wrapped him in his country's tricolour flag, and then the celebrations were cut short as overjoyed City fans invaded the pitch. No-one begrudged those supporters. This was their moment.

Mancini, still wrapped in the Italian flag, beat a hasty retreat down the tunnel to evade the supporters who wanted to kiss, cuddle and back-slap, and walked straight into a bear hug from his elderly father Aldo. It was an emotional moment, as Mancini junior has spent every available spare moment travelling back to his home town of Jesi, since his dad had a heart attack in July 2010.

Mancini later admitted that he had been momentarily afraid for his father's health as he watched such nerve-jangling drama from the stands. But Aldo was just delighted for his son, and for his country, seeing it as a matter of national pride as well as family joy.

Then Roberto hugged his two boys, Andrea and Filippo – who were both on City's books as players at the time – and made his way outside for the trophy presentation, joining the general mayhem in the back corridors of the stadium. There were similar scenes with mother Marianna, younger sister Stefania, wife Federica and daughter Camilla.

Once the pitch was clear, the stage-managed trophy presentation took place and after the obligatory drenching in champagne by his players, Mancini shared a few quiet words with some of them, most notably with Carlos Tevez. The two men had been portrayed as bitter enemies just weeks earlier, unwilling and unable ever to work together again. In September 2011, Mancini had vowed that Tevez was "finished" at City after the two men clashed over the Argentine striker's refusal to leave the substitutes' bench and resume his warm-up in a Champions League group fixture at Bayern Munich. Their relationship had spiralled downwards from that moment, and Tevez had, sensationally, walked out on the club and flown home to be with his friends and family in Argentina. It seemed that the whole sordid affair was heading for an equally messy ending, with talk of the club suing the player.

In the end, a truce was called, Tevez returned and, ignoring accusations of hypocrisy and desperation, Mancini had welcomed the prodigal player back into his squad, with invigorating effects. As they stood on the turf at the Etihad Stadium, league winners' medals around their necks, sharing a few friendly words, it appeared that the sorry episode had engendered new respect, reinforced by the victory.

But already the flush of success was fading for Mancini. He is one of those sportsmen who strive to reach the stars, and no sooner have they arrived than they are casting covetous eyes at the next galaxy along.

The air was heavy with significance and symbolism, even as City fans began a party which gave their United workmates hangovers. The Premier League trophy had been carried onto the pitch by surviving members of the 1968 City team that had last won the title. After forming a guard of honour, the legends, headed by Colin Bell, Francis Lee and Mike Summerbee, duly trooped off the field to ensure that the modern-day heroes took the limelight.

Summerbee, still an ambassador for the club, was aware of the symbolism. "With all respect, we had started to get a bit fed up of people talking about Bell, Lee and Summerbee," he said. "Me and the other boys from 1968 carried the trophy onto to the field, and the crowd was clapping us as we went off. I knew then that the door had closed on that era. We had been locked away in the history of the football club. There is a new generation now, and they can go on from this and be very successful."

Mancini was drained, physically and emotionally, paying the price for a season which had begun with brilliance, dipped into doubt and ended with astounding fortitude and good fortune. He still had time to reflect on what had gone on, to try to make sense of those five bizarre minutes.

Carrying the Premier League trophy together with his captain Vincent Kompany, Mancini entered the post-match press conference to loud, heartfelt applause. He has won many admirers in the English media, especially those based in Manchester, as he offers a stark contrast to the irascible and confrontational United manager Sir Alex Ferguson. And as his confidence in his own assimilation into English football culture has grown, he has revealed an impish sense of humour, and a willingness to answer any question, no matter how impertinent.

The first question after the applause had died down was a cheeky reference to Mancini's refusal first to accept that his team was back in the hunt, and second, after beating United in a tense derby at the Etihad, to acknowledge that his side had regained the initiative.

"Roberto, now do you accept that you are favourites for the title?" said the beaming journalist, and Mancini appreciated the joke.

Then he reflected on the madness of the match in which he had just taken part. He is not eloquent in English, and prefers his players to do his talking for him out on the pitch, but at times his words are tellingly accurate. He admitted that as the game entered time added on, the best he dared to hope was that his team could score an equalizer and that Sunderland might do the same. Both games would be drawn, and City would take the title.

"I hoped always that Sunderland could score and draw," he said. "For this reason, it was important for us to score and draw. It was a crazy finish to a crazy season. I have never seen a finale like this. We have changed the history of this club, and for this we should be proud."

But if anyone was about to dare to suggest that "grazia" had played its part, and that Lady Luck might have helped Aguero's thunderbolt shot on its way, Mancini was adamant. The title had not been won in that moment. It had been earned over nine months of hard slog, and no-one was going to deny that City were fitting champions, just because they had snatched an unlikely victory right at the death.

"We deserved to win the title," he said. "I've never seen a moment like this. In the history of the club a finale like this doesn't exist. I'm very proud of my players because I think that they wanted to win this title. They worked hard for this and they wanted to win the title until the last second of the last game.

"The best team won the title, for sure. We played the best football, we conceded fewer goals and scored more goals, we beat United two times. We scored more goals than them and conceded fewer goals than them. We deserved to win, and to beat a strong team like United is fantastic."

More than anything, Mancini's initial task, of building a team with the kind of winning mentality which had sustained United for so long, had clearly been completed.

"We have big character," he said. "If not, it would have been impossible to recover in this game and score two goals in two minutes in the last game. We wanted this title with all our strength."

The critics persisted with their wearisome mantra, claiming that City had bought the title, and that Mancini was a passenger rather than a pilot on the flight to success. It was nonsense. Of course the oil money had greased the cogs of triumph for the Blues, but it is a fact of Premier League life that you need money, and more of it than the majority, in order to lift the big prizes. If City had bought the title, so had United, Blackburn, Arsenal and Chelsea before them. And to belittle Mancini's contribution makes as much sense as playing down the roles played by Sir Alex Ferguson, Arsène Wenger and José Mourinho in recent years, all of whom spent liberally in pursuit of the biggest prize in English football.

Being replete with riches brings its own problems. Big players have big egos, all with their own ideas about how the team should play, who should play. That had been evident at City, where big names like Robinho, Emmanuel Adebayor and Craig Bellamy had come and gone, leaving barely a ripple.

The same people who accused City of buying the title had also derided the Blues as a collection of mercenaries, only there for the money. At the height of the title battle, United coach René Meulensteen, one of Ferguson's right-hand men, had made this distinction, hinting that the Blues were a bunch of egomaniacs, and that United would win the title as they were a team, not burdened by mavericks like Balotelli.

Chapter One

"City do not have a well-balanced team", said the Dutchman. "They only have individuals who play for themselves. You can see that City lack the right team spirit. There is no chance of Balotelli playing for Manchester United. A player who gets up to the antics he does has no place at our club. I don't believe that Sir Alex would sign a player like Balotelli. We shouldn't get in people like him – they only bring frustration.

"United are accustomed to the pressure involved in going for the title. City are in a position to win the league for the first time in a long while, but that is breaking them up. I thought they wouldn't hold out to the end."

Meulensteen's diatribe was both premature and wrong. The fact that City did not just "hold out", but won the title with a run of six straight victories as United crumbled, was an eloquent answer to the Dutchman. Mancini had indeed moulded his players into a team, given them a shape and pattern within which the world-class talents of David Silva, Yaya Touré and Sergio Aguero could flourish.

The decision to re-integrate Tevez had been widely criticized, not least by Ferguson himself, who had described it as "desperate". But when Mancini brought the wayward Argentine back, he knew that regardless of his own chequered history with the player, "Carlito" was well liked and respected in the dressing-room.

It was a big call. City legend Rodney Marsh suggested on national radio that if City failed to win the title after bringing back Tevez, it would cost Mancini his job. Regardless of the morals involved, however, and the fact that many Blues fans were unhappy at seeing Tevez pull on the shirt again, it turned out to be a master-stroke. Tevez reinvigorated a side that was clearly flagging, bringing energy and determination high up the field, not to mention dollops of ability and a fruitful partnership with his countryman Aguero.

***

There can be no doubt that the money on offer was attractive to Mancini when he joined City in December 2009. He instantly became one of the top three managers in the country in terms of salary. But the challenge of turning the Blues from a middling English club, prone to gaffe and disaster, into English champions and a European force, was also a strong motivation. It had been a recurring theme in his career, spurning the lure of the glamour clubs and instead electing to help the unfashionable become sexy.

As an Italy international and one of the most gifted players of his generation, Mancini could have taken his pick of the big clubs. Instead, he left his first club Bologna for Sampdoria, helping them to Serie A, Coppa Italia and European glory, and moved on to Lazio. For an Italian star to avoid the glamour clubs AC Milan and Juventus and play out his career in comparative football backwaters could sometimes be a sign of fear, the worry that he would be a small fish in those shark-infested waters. That charge could never be levelled at Mancini. He revelled in the opportunity to challenge the established giants.

It was the same when he became a manager. Always marked down as management material, not least by his last manager in Italy, Sven-Goran Eriksson, he took the reins at Fiorentina, a club beset by financial troubles, and won the Italian cup. He then had another stricken club, Lazio, punching above its weight, before moving to Internazionale.

Just as when he moved to Manchester, he took over a club which had been trophy-less for longer than its fans cared to remember, and had that wound repeatedly salted by the success of their city rivals AC Milan. Again he broke the hoodoo, raking in a hat-trick of Serie A titles and doing much of the groundwork which would allow Mourinho to take them to Champions League glory.

But taking on City, long-term basket-cases of English football, was a whole new challenge. He had fallen in love with English football's pace and passion during a strange swansong to his playing career at Leicester City. The chance to turn around the fortunes of an under-achieving club in an alien football culture appealed to his sense of wanting to challenge himself.

Rival boss Sir Alex Ferguson had vowed, on assuming control of United, to knock Liverpool "off their f****ing perch" – he had done so and ushered in a new dynasty. Mancini's immediate promise had been more modest, but just as emotive, and hit just the right buttons for City supporters itching for the club to use its new-found wealth and power to put one over on the Reds, who they deem decadent and arrogant.

United fans had for years mocked City's long barren years with a milometer-style banner hung at the Stretford End. When Mancini assumed control at City, that banner simply read "33 Years", measuring the time since the Blues won the League Cup in 1976.

"When we go to Old Trafford we will take that banner down," said Mancini. The boast was met with derision by United fans, and it was one of the reasons Ferguson himself described the renascent City as "noisy neighbours", but it was the right thing to say at the right time. City fans wanted a man who would stand up to Ferguson, who had grown used to getting his own way.

Mancini made good his vow in May 2011, leading his City side to FA Cup triumph. The Stretford End banner, which had by then been changed to "34 Years", was quietly removed. The United supporters responsible for it briefly discussed the idea of replacing it with a "43 Years" banner to signify the amount of time since City had last won the league. But even they realized that the tide had turned, and that any further mockery would be akin to King Canute shouting at the waves as they rolled over him.

City then proceeded to adopt the idea for themselves. When the trophy was lifted skywards at the Etihad, the stadium scoreboards showed a facsimile of the deceased banner, standing at "44 Years" and then counting down to "00 Years", to huge cheers.

Mancini had met United on their own terms and now here he was, two years and five months after taking over from Mark Hughes, standing at the pinnacle of English football and eyeing loftier peaks. Sweetest of all for City fans was the poetic fact that City had won the title courtesy of their stunning 6–1 win at Old Trafford on October 23, 2011. They pipped United to the post because their goal difference was better by eight. Had they not rubbed Red noses in it on that eye-opening autumn day, the title might have remained with their hated rivals.

Such matters are trivia to Mancini. He is not interested in the minutiae which make up victories, but in the victories themselves. On their way to title success, City had broken the Premier League record for consecutive home wins, by winning 20 on the trot in a run which began in the previous season. And Aguero's goal on the final day of the season made him the first City player since Francis Lee in 1972 to have bagged 30 goals in a season.

Mancini greets such milestones with barely a flicker of recognition. He measures success by the number and quality of trophies in the cabinet. Everything else is irrelevant, and to mention such trivia in his presence is to evoke a look of ill-concealed disregard. He has barely glanced at City's past, preferring to dedicate himself to their future, and maybe fearing that the curse of Typical City might also infect him if he looks too closely. But City's past, good and bad, is everywhere, even at the ten-year-old Etihad Stadium, as their fans are proud of their heritage and revel in their own loyalty during the hard years. Maybe that has been Mancini's greatest triumph, banishing the spectre of Typical City at the very moment when it appeared to have played its greatest and dirtiest trick on the club.

The writing had been on the wall for that shade of the past. This team had reversed the Blues' traditional process of snatching defeat from the jaws of triumph. They had come from behind to record their first-ever Champions League win in October, as Aguero scored a winner in the third minute of added time. Mario Balotelli had won and scored a late penalty to beat Tottenham 3–2 in January, and they had scored twice in the last five minutes to retrieve a point at home to Sunderland in March, a point which felt useless at the time but was to prove precious. Typical City is now beginning to assume positive aspects, rather than conveying ridiculousness or hapless failure.

Not that Mancini will rest there. He is already planning to turn one league title win into two, and will no doubt have an eye on matching his own Serie A feat of securing a hat-trick of titles. Next time however, he wants to do it in a fashion which is a little easier on the nerves.

"It's important that we win a second title before another 44 years passes," he said. "We need to recover and next season we can talk about the future. Doing it like this is very hard and I hope it's the last time for us. Next year, it's important to win it one game before the end.

"I hope that we can continue to win things, but we need to improve. In two years we have improved a lot, but we need to improve next year in the championship and in the Champions League. We have to play in two competitions at the same level."

Chapter Two
Teenage Sensation

Sneaking out of his first Holy Communion, eight-year-old Roberto Mancini was a boy on a mission. His team, Aurora, was losing a match and needed its star player, even if he was in the middle of one of the most important days of his young life. He stole away, quickly changed into his boots, turned the game around and then slipped back to church again. But he had been spotted. His dad Aldo had noticed that Roberto was missing from the service and, embarrassed, approached the priest, Father Roberto Vigo, to apologize for his errant offspring. The priest, a little shame-faced, admitted that he had put young Mancini up to it.

Father Vigo was also the boy's first football coach, and it was he who had suggested the quick change when he heard that his team were losing! As a boy, Mancini had two passions – the church and football. He was an altar boy at the San Sebastian church and a promising footballer for Aurora, the club based next door to the church and across the road from the flat where his parents still live in the town of Jesi. It was a trinity – church, family and football – which sustained the young Roberto then, and still does.

"Like most boys in the area, Roberto's life revolved around football and religion," Aldo recalls. "He was always playing football at the Aurora Calcio. As soon as he came home from school he would be over there, kicking a ball with his friends. There was no stopping him. It was always football, football, football. He used to sleep with his football. The only time he didn't have a football with him was when he was carrying out his duties as an altar boy. But then as soon as he was finished at church on Sunday morning, he would change into his football kit and go to the pitch next door to play a match."

***

Mancini was born on November 27, 1964 in Jesi, a small, quiet town in the province of Ancona, 20 miles inland from Italy's Adriatic coast. His parents are Aldo Mancini, a joiner, and his wife Marianna, a nurse from the town of Roccadaspide, south of Naples. The couple met when Aldo was on holiday in southern Italy as a young man and settled in Aldo's home town of Jesi, where they raised Roberto and his younger sister Stephanie.

Like Father Vigo, Aldo was also prepared to bend the rules for his son – he told Aurora that five-year-old Roberto was six in order to circumvent the club rules on minimum age and give him an early start on the road to football stardom. By the time he was 13, it was plain that young Roberto's destiny was far greater than being the star of his local football team. He had his eyes opened by accompanying dad Aldo on the 12-hour, 680-mile round trip to Turin to watch Juventus play, and occasionally to see their city rivals Torino. The boy Mancini's idols were the great Juve strikers Roberto Boninsegna and Roberto Bettega. On the playing side, Aldo would always be behind Roberto, coaxing and cajoling him on to better things, and even now he can feel the sharp edge of Aldo's tongue if he makes a mistake:

"My father has always been my biggest critic both as a manager and when I was a player," said Roberto. "He criticized me every time I played. But this is important because if your father says these things it means they are true. And for me it is important to improve, always. He was my first supporter and he pushed me in football."

Perhaps that is an insight into Mancini's own reluctance to praise many of the young players under his charge at City. Invited to talk about bright performances from the likes of Joe Hart, Adam Johnson and James Milner, he frequently plays down their contribution, and invariably ends with the sentence: "He needs to improve." Mancini knows from his own experience of his dad's hypercritical approach that a lack of praise can be more motivating for a confident, ambitious youngster than gushing tributes.

Aldo's brand of encouragement and perfectionism fired young Mancini's dreams, and by the time he was 13, his dad had charged family friend Alberto Marchetti to take him to Bologna's Casteldebole training complex. Although he was a Juve fan, Bologna was the closest Serie A team to his Jesi home, and Mancini knew the stories of the 1963–64 team which had been the last "Rossoblu" (red and blue) team to win the league title – tales of midfielder Roman Fogli and winger Marino Perani, both of whom went on to represent their country at the 1966 World Cup finals. Perani also starred in the Bologna team which knocked Manchester City out of the 1970–71 Anglo-Italian Cup.

By the time Mancini made the move to Bologna, Perani was in charge of the youth team and he was quick to spot the potential of the young boy from Jesi. Legend has it that AC Milan had also taken an interest, and sent a telegram inviting young Mancini to their Milanello training complex. Unfortunately for them, they sent it to the wrong Jesi club, or the history of Italian football might have been different!

Even the lesser charms of Bologna had Mancini dreaming of glory: "I remember the strong emotion that accompanied me when I got to Casteldebole for the fateful audition," said Mancini. "The legendary Bologna of Perani and Fogli … a dream. It was an unforgettable moment. I was very young and it was hard, the first year."

Bologna was over two hours' drive from Jesi, and the young Roberto had to leave the comfort and closeness of his family if he wanted to pursue his dream: "My sons are older now, but if I think of them when they were 13, I could not imagine them leaving home. But football was my priority and it changed me."

The Bologna coaches, headed by talent spotter supreme Walter Bicocchi, were blown away by Mancini's ability and handed over 500,000 lira – about £500 – to Aurora as a thank you for pointing the young talent in their direction, with the promise of another £3,500 if he made it to the first team. Such was his potential that he was soon training with the 16-year-olds, boys two years older than him, but he was more than holding his own. It was at this middling Serie A club that Mancini acquired his love of the underdog. Bologna have won seven Italian league titles, the last in 1964, although their last major trophy was the 1974 Coppa Italia, just three years before the bright-eyed boy from Jesi walked through the door.

They were very much on the slide when Mancini joined them, changing coaches at the drop of a hat; when the first-team coach Tarcisio Burgnich decided to hurl the young Mancini into the physically tough, technically demanding Serie A fray in the 1981–82 season, it may have been out of desperation as much as insight. Mancini was just 16, but former Inter and Italy defender Burgnich knew he had a special talent on his hands. The boy had carried on his studies alongside his training at Casteldebole, learning to be a surveyor, but few thought he would ever need skills other than those he showed on a football pitch.

The previous coach, Luigi Radice, had seen the player make his debut in the Primavera, the youth championship for Serie A clubs, and invited him to join a few first-team training sessions. He knew he had a star on his hands. The slender kid was quick, had great feet and close control, and was a deadly finisher – in the season before his debut, Mancini had scored 45 goals in 28 appearances for the Bologna youth team and helped them to win the national youth title for the first time. Bologna had high hopes for that season, as they had finished seventh in Serie A in 1980–81 despite being deducted five points for their part in a match-fixing scandal. Burgnich handed the youngster his debut in a Coppa Italia (Italian Cup) group game against Reggina on September 6, 1981. It was fitting that his debut in senior football should be in that competition, as he went on to make a record 120 appearances in it, and won it six times as a player and four as a coach.

Just a week later, Mancini made his bow in Serie A, coming on for the last few minutes of the 1–1 draw with Cagliari on September 13, 1981. That call-up came as a big surprise. Burgnich had to argue with president Tommaso Fabbretti for permission to play the boy, as the club had already arranged for him to go on loan to Serie B side Forli to gain experience. Mancini's senior debut was so sudden that his dad Aldo had travelled to Rimini to watch his son play in the youth team, only to find out that he would be playing for the first team – he made it to the Stadio Comunale, 75 miles away, with minutes to spare.

The notion of sending Mancini out on loan was soon ditched as he became Bologna's principal weapon in an ultimately unsuccessful fight against relegation. The following month Mancini grabbed his first senior goal, scoring the 78th-minute equalizer to complete a comeback to 2–2 from 2–0 down to Como. At the time he was earning the princely sum of £40 a month – and sending most of it back to his parents.

"He played in midfield, a bit like Michel Platini towards the end," said Burgnich of the young prodigy's only season in the red and blue. "He dictated the rhythm of a game and had a great sense of timing when it came to getting forward. Despite being the youngest guy in the team he was already a leader, but at that time you could never have foreseen his future as a manager. He was a sensitive boy, not very expansive, and I think his personality blossomed later on. He was good at adapting his characteristics to the team. I, for example, needed a striker and he scored nine goals. And to think that just to have him I had to have a huge argument with the president, Tommaso Fabbretti, who had already promised him on loan to Forli."

In his debut season, his only campaign for Bologna, the club struggled but Mancini flourished. The young newcomer made 31 appearances, 25 of them from the start, and scored nine times to give the fans a new hero and fresh hope for the future. He would later curse that season, however, as it pigeon-holed him as a striker, and he always preferred to play in midfield.

It wasn't just the goals that made everyone sit up and take notice, it was the quality and the composure which attended them. Outstanding examples included a beautifully cushioned side-foot volley in the bear-pit of Roma and a sharp burst of pace, exquisite touch and laser-accurate finish in the home fixture against the same team, and it became plain that there was a new star rising in the firmament of Italian football. One Bologna fan wrote that Mancini "appeared like a comet in the sky of the red and blues" – but the old superstition that comets are harbingers of doom, and are all too often gone in a flash, proved all too true for the hopeful Bologna fans.

They had been one of only three Italian clubs never to have been out of the top flight, along with Juventus and Inter, but in 1982 they suffered the first relegation in their history. Their sporting director, Paolo Borea, left to take up the same post at Genoa club Sampdoria and urged his new club's president, Paolo Mantovani, to move quickly for the precocious teenager. Mantovani, who would become a central figure in Mancini's life, took notice. The fee for "Mancio", as he was nicknamed, was staggering – cash plus three Sampdoria players and a loan signing went in the other direction. The deal has since been valued at £2.2 million, an astonishing figure for a 17-year-old.

It was a terrible double blow for the Bologna fans, who had seen their team relegated and lost their brightest hope for the future within weeks. They marched through the streets of the town, smashed the windows of president Fabbretti's insurance business and even conspired to burn his house down. But for Mancini himself it was a case of onwards and upwards, as he had joined a new rising force in Italian football. Sampdoria had been middling achievers in Italian football, having never won a major trophy. Then, in 1979, the "Blucerchiati" – the nickname roughly translates as "blue with circles", a reference to their azure shirts with a black, red and white hoop – were taken over by oil millionaire Mantovani, and their fortunes took a turn for the better.

He invested in the team, notably with that astonishing fee for young Mancini, and as Bologna were being relegated, Sampdoria were passing them in the other direction after five seasons in Serie B. The money they gambled on the exciting teenager proved to be the best investment they ever made, as he was the driving force which turned them from an unfashionable provincial club into one which would challenge the dominance of the big-city glamour clubs Juventus, AC Milan and Internazionale. Mancini would stay for 15 seasons, setting new appearance and goalscoring records for the club and leading them to their only Serie A title, plus four Coppa Italias and a European Cup Winners' Cup. Sampdoria had some great players in that era – Gianluca Vialli, Toninho Cerezo, Attilio Lombardo, Graeme Souness, David Platt and Trevor Francis among them – but it was Mancini who came to symbolize their success and establish himself as their greatest player.

The fact that he resisted a move to one of the big clubs, or abroad to one of the Spanish giants, tells you something about Mancini's psyche. It was not due to a fear of not being able to cut it in the rarefied atmosphere of one of the world's top outfits – he had the self-confidence and the ability to play anywhere. But the romance and the challenge of transforming Sampdoria appealed to his sense of destiny, and his love of a challenge, far more than simply moving to a club where silverware and glory were guaranteed. For that reason, Mancini holds a place of affection among many Italian football fans, especially those who support the lesser lights.

When he visited Napoli with Manchester City in the Champions League in 2011, the respect felt for him was tangible, and not just because his mother is from the region. Always dismissive of the rich, aloof northern clubs, Neapolitans recognized Mancini's decision to resist their lure and their riches and instead fight on the side of the underdog.

The teenage Mancini had the size of his task at Sampdoria vividly mapped out for him. Mantovani had splashed out £700,000 to buy another striker, Trevor Francis from Manchester City, fresh from appearing at the 1982 World Cup finals for England. Mancini, despite his fee, slipped into Sampdoria under the radar by comparison. The presentation of Francis to the fanatical Samp fans brought Genoa city centre grinding to a halt for three hours – it was a real sign that Mantovani and coach Renzo Ulivieri meant business. It was also fierce competition and, despite his tender years, Mancini quickly proved he was no great respecter of reputations.

Mancini soon got frustrated with his new coach, Ulivieri. Mancini was special as a player, and combined with his outspoken nature, it made him a formidable foe for any coach, or referee, with whom he crossed swords. But his new career was off to an inauspicious start. During his first season at Marassi – as the Stadio Luigi Ferraris is usually called, after the district in which it stands – Mancini scored just five goals in 27 games. Ulivieri used him not as an attacking midfielder, or "trequartista" as the Italians call it, but as an out-and-out striker.

The coach recalls an exchange with Mancini shortly after the shy, fresh-faced youngster joined Samp. "You, boy, what role do you play?" asked the 41-year-old boss.

"I like playing behind the strikers, at a distance," came the reply.

"And you scored nine goals for Bologna starting from a distance? You are a central striker and that is where you will play for me."

That created an instant problem between the two men, as the teenager was strong-willed and sure of himself, and felt he knew best.

The fans in Genoa were left wondering what all the fuss was about, although their team finished an impressive seventh place in their first season back in the top flight. Mancini was indignant. He later said: "I was a midfielder who for reasons of necessity had been deployed up front."

Mancini also began his long love affair with the Coppa Italia by scoring his first Sampdoria goal in a 4–0 win over Brescia on September 1, 1982. Eleven days later he was making his first start for the club in Serie A, against his boyhood heroes Juventus, helping his new team to a 1–0 win. He announced himself in great style in his next game, scoring the winner as Sampdoria shocked Inter 2–1 at the San Siro, and netted the only goal the following week as Roma – who would finish the season as champions – were dispatched at Marassi. Francis, who had a reputation of fragility in his time at Manchester City and would also be dogged by injuries throughout his time in Genoa, tore a hamstring in the Roma game, and suddenly the goalscoring burden rested largely on Mancini's slender shoulders.

In October 1982, Mancini also embarked on his international career – which was to prove ultimately unfulfilling – with a call-up for Italy's under-21 team, even though he was still 17. That meant he was to play at that level for four seasons, racking up almost as many appearances as he did for the senior national team.

At first he appeared untroubled by the sudden elevation to club and national importance, making it three goals in three games the following week, in a 3–2 defeat at Pisa, and then marking his 18th birthday by scoring in the derby match at Genoa. That was to be his last goal of the season, and for the first time in his life, Mancini had to question himself, and his coach, as he found himself gnawing on his own enthusiasm, spending time on the bench. He was an 18-

year-old rookie and Francis was a 29-year-old with vast international experience who had become English football's first million-pound footballer in 1979, but the young Italian was prepared to fight for his place – literally, on one occasion.

Since joining Manchester City, Mancini has been unfazed by a series of training ground clashes between his City stars, which were portrayed as evidence that his squad were at war with each other. Mancini was cool about those bust-ups, and recalled his own fiery clashes on the training ground, not least with Francis, for whom he actually had great respect, and says is the best British player to have plied his trade in Italy. When asked about City's training-ground scraps, Mancini said: "I had these about five times. One time when I was young I had a fight in training against an English player who was playing with me at Sampdoria – Trevor Francis. I don't remember the cause of it, because it was about 25 years ago, but I remember very well the fight. It's important that after it was finished we made friends."

Francis also remembers it well: "It happened about a year after I got there," he said. "There was a little incident in a friendly training match that at the time I thought was something and nothing. We had a disagreement on the pitch about it but it continued into the dressing-room. We had to be split from each other. Let's just say all the players made sure that it didn't go any further. We made up afterwards and there was no ill feeling, after all we played together for another three years." Mancini also had a punch-up with Arsenal legend Liam Brady, another of the star names brought in by Mantovani, after he was moved out of Juventus to make way for Michel Platini.

The feeling going into Mancini's second season was that if Samp could keep Francis fit they could make a more serious assault on the

Scudetto, the Italian name for their league title, meaning shield. They had added title-winning experience in the shape of Italy goalkeeper Ivano Bordon, from Inter, and a brute of a defender, Pietro Vierchowod, fresh from winning the trophy with Roma. But injury problems again afflicted Francis, who played only 22 games, scoring five goals. That was Mancini's cue, and he was an ever-present, finishing the season as top scorer with ten goals.

The young Mancini was not impressed with Ulivieri, however, and even less so when he was left on the bench. He later said of his coach: "He lacks cunning and is too spontaneous. And in that job you have to know how to pretend." Ulivieri had no chance. Mantovani loved Mancini from the first time he saw him play, and came to treat him like a son – the player even asked the president to look after his earnings for him.

Early TV interviews with Mancini appear to show a shy, softly-spoken boy, someone from a provincial town thrust into an unwanted spotlight. But that façade hid a driven individual, a man who was not going to allow his genius to be denied by anyone – and that included coaches and referees, who both felt the full force of his fury at times in his career. Whether Mancini had any say in the removal of Ulivieri in 1984 is unclear, although he later spoke of his feelings about the matter. "I was a strong player and got left out. It was difficult for me because it was the start of my career," he said. "He kept me on the bench and I was angry and frustrated. Every day you must work to convince the manager to change his decision."

So what did he do about it? "Change manager!" said Mancini, with a beaming grin and twinkling eye.

Ulivieri moved on to Cagliari, to be replaced by Eugenio Bersellini, a coach known as the Iron Sergeant. The highlight of his extensive coaching career was to guide Inter to the Scudetto in 1980. Bersellini lived up to his nickname, introducing a strict training regime at Samp, and like Ulivieri he was soon rubbing the young Mancini up the wrong way. He had little time for "flash" players like Mancini, and he resented the fact that in his view Mancini did not defend enough.

"Mancini had rare qualities in terms of technique, and I never doubted that," Bersellini said. "But he needed to channel it from a tactical point of view. I wanted him to come back when the opposition had the ball. I did everything to shake him out of it, but did not get far. He was resisting and became more and more closed."

In spite of the player's resistance, perhaps some of the lessons Bersellini tried to instil did rub off, as Mancini has had the same battles at City, notably with Adam Johnson, a skilful winger who has not always fulfilled his defensive duties – and found himself out of the team because of it. Mancini has even admitted being "lazy" as a young player.

What is more, Bersellini delivered. In the summer of 1984, Samp brought in the experience of Graeme Souness, a European Cup winner with Liverpool, for £650,000, and a bright 20-year-old striker named Gianluca Vialli from Cremonese, as well as recalling playmaker Fausto Salsano from Parma, where he had spent two seasons on loan. That began a friendship which endures to this day, as Salsano is a coach and trusted confidant of Mancini at City. Brady left to join Inter, and a Samp team which was a nice blend of rugged experience and thrusting youth equalled their highest Serie A finish, taking fourth place. They also won their first major honour, lifting the Coppa Italia. In a two-legged final, Souness gave Samp a valuable 1–0 away win over AC Milan at the San Siro with a far-post volley from a Francis cross. Mancini sat on the bench for an hour before replacing the injured Francis.

In the return, in front of a disbelieving capacity crowd at Marassi, Mancini virtually settled it with an ice-cool penalty in the first half, before Vialli made it 3–0 on aggregate with a brilliant second-half goal. Pietro Paolo Virdis pulled one back, but the Samp fans were in ecstasy, and – like City supporters after the FA Cup victory 26 years later – were already dreaming of bigger prizes.

By contrast, the 20-year-old Mancini felt he was going backwards after scoring just three goals that season. Winning his first major honour, and getting his first international cap against Canada in the summer of 1984, was scant consolation for the impatient youngster. He wanted to be at the heart of things, and felt he was getting nowhere under Bersellini. Mancini was later unequivocal in his views on the coach: "With him, I lost two years. Eventually I asked Mantovani to ask him if I could go on loan to Bologna in Serie B. I know a manager must give a team his own footprint, but that shouldn't mean caging the imagination of certain players."

The two men also clashed over Mancini's predilection for the back-heel, which would become a trademark of his play. The stern old coach didn't like the idea of it, but Mancini's view, perhaps designed to infuriate, was "If my team-mate is behind me, why should I make the effort to turn around?"

Mancini and Vialli had shown their potential but, when he was not injured, Francis was still the main man. His nine goals made him not only the top scorer in the Coppa Italia that season, but also the only Englishman ever to top any goalscoring chart in Italy. Bersellini brought in Giuseppe Lorenzo, a striker with a proven goal record in the lower divisions, to bring the complement of strikers up to four, and in 1985–86 he rotated between him, Francis – still cursed by injury troubles – Mancini and Vialli. Mancini top-scored with 12 goals in 27 appearances, but only half of them were in the league, and after the promise of the previous season, Samp disappointingly finished in 11th place.

Other clubs, notably Pisa, Avellino, Roma, Verona and Torino, were interested as Mancini's disaffection became apparent. Meanwhile, at the age of 20, he had his first experience of European football in the autumn of 1985, and scored in both legs as Samp progressed past the Cup Winners' Cup first round with a 2–1 aggregate win over Greek side Larissa. They went out to Benfica in the next round, and it was to be a disappointing season for Samp, culminating in defeat in the Coppa Italia final by Sven-Goran Eriksson's Roma. Mancini scored as the Blucerchiati took a 2–1 lead in the first leg, but they slumped to a 2–0 defeat in the second leg at the Stadio Olimpico.

That was enough to see the back of Bersellini, and it couldn't come soon enough for Mancini. The replacement was Serb coach and former Sampdoria player Vujadin Boskov. He was known as a "gypsy" coach, whose 24 years in coaching had taken him to Switzerland, Serbia, Holland and Spain before he returned to Italy. The new coach did not find Mancini easy to get along with at first, but he was smarter and more circumspect in dealing with the talented young star. Years later, when Mancini, as Inter manager, had a long-standing feud with Luis Figo, Boskov had a wry smile to himself, and expressed the view that Mancio should know better. "He has certainly not learned how to handle a star player from me," he said. "In that sense he has to be a little bit more flexible. After all, Roberto was not an easy player to deal with himself."

Still, at least there was mutual respect between Mancini and his new coach, and he felt his career was back on track. He credits Boskov with teaching him that innate ability alone will not make you a top player, that it needs to be allied to serious graft. "When I started my career, I didn't work hard," he said. "I thought if you have good quality, you can play for a top team and at the maximum level. But if you don't work every day, you don't improve. I worked with Vujadin Boskov and Sven-Goran Eriksson for many years. These two managers changed my mind."

Boskov hit on the formula for dealing with Mancini. He let Mantovani, who had a father-son relationship with the player, deal with the outbursts, while he stuck strictly to coaching and improving the team, and the player. Mancini was far happier; it showed in his game, and he revealed his pleasure at the time: "Under Bersellini, during training you could hear a pin drop. When Boskov came, everything was reborn. Now I cannot wait to start training because we have fun, joke around, and every day the old fox has a way of surprising us, of making us sweat with joy. He is a man who gives you a lot of confidence, helps you believe in yourself. And off the field, he always knows if you have a problem and tries to solve it, maybe at a bar, offering you drinks."

Perhaps another trick he learned from Boskov was the art of the banal quote. Italian football is renowned for its over-analysis, as the legions of football journalists try to fill hours of TV time and column inches, and the Serb rarely strayed away from the deadly dull, much to the amusement of pressmen and football people alike. "Football is football" was a favourite, along with "I think we need to shoot on goal to score". Mancini is now a master of Boskov's art, partly as a means to avoid landing himself in hot water, partly due to his lack of confidence in his own English, and partly out of boredom at the endless rounds of media interviews.

Francis and Souness moved on in the summer of 1987, but Boskov brought in Brazilian star Toninho Cerezo and felt his team now had the ability to mix it with the big boys. His words were borne out in 1987–88 as Samp finished fourth and won the Coppa Italia for the second time, beating Torino 2–0 in the first leg of the final and, after throwing away the lead in the second leg, winning it in extra time through Salsano's great strike.

At the age of 23, and now in tandem with Vialli, Mancini appeared to have the world at his feet, ready to expand his horizons at the 1988 European Championships by becoming an ascendant star on the international scene as well as a Serie A hero. After a couple of costly brushes with authority, Mancini had knuckled back down to his football, and was happier than at any time in his career. He spoke of signing a new ten-year contract if it was offered and of coaching Sampdoria once his career was over. With the trophies starting to roll into Marassi, his international career re-launched, and his first big international tournament on the horizon, things looked rosy for Roberto.

Mancini's ultimately disappointing international career is dealt with in the next chapter, but it was in domestic Italian football that his legend was made. Sampdoria were a small fish in a very big pond in the late 1980s, when Italian football was a magnet for the world's greatest players. Legends like Diego Maradona, Ruud Gullit, Jurgen Klinsmann, Lothar Matthaus and Marco van Basten flocked to Serie A. None of them went to Samp.

Boskov and his sporting director Paolo Borea put their faith in bringing in lesser international stars and the best young Italian talent. The arrival of Beppe Dossena was perhaps the catalyst for the team. Both Vialli and Mancini urged the club to sign the 31-year-old former Italy international, believing he could help to turn Samp from a good team into a great one. Vialli and Mancini were seen by many as the real power at Sampdoria at that time, in cohorts with president Mantovani, and there were numerous stories of them ordering substitutions, picking out players for transfer – in or out – and organizing tactics.

Some of the stories are true, but Vialli later said that the extent of their influence was exaggerated: "Some people claimed Mancini and I put the team together, but in reality it was Boskov. Just before the [1992 Champions League] final Mancini and I went to Boskov to give him some advice on tactics. As usual, he just said, 'Yes, yes, yes' – and then went and did exactly what he wanted."

Mancini, Vialli, Vierchowod, goalkeeper Gianluca Pagliua and a few other Samp players could have made the club a fortune, if they had followed the well-trodden paths from the lesser lights of Serie A to the big clubs, but the proposed sale of Vialli to AC Milan in 1986, for over £4 million, had fallen through when the outraged Vialli refused to leave.

President Mantovani was already a rich man, loved his team, and treated his players like sons. In turn, they revered him like a father, and revelled in the beautiful if flawed team that he had put together. The football was stylish, Samp had a growing cult following outside of Genoa, and even outside of Italy, and the players would often be seen dining together in the quayside restaurant La Piedigrotta, talking of tactics, joking, laughing and contemplating future glory.

Samp had already shown they were a force to be reckoned with, winning the 1988 Coppa Italia, and the following year lifting it again as well as reaching the club's first European final, when they lost to Barcelona in the Cup Winners' Cup. Vialli was the goalscoring hero in the European campaign, scoring five times in six games as Samp eased past Norrkoping, Carl Zeiss Jena and Dinamo Bucharest and then saw off defending champions Mechelen in a tense semi-final. After a 2–1 defeat in Belgium in the first leg, Samp struck three times in the last 19 minutes through Cerezo, Dossena and Fausto Salsano to reach the final and send the 40,000 Marassi crowd into delirium.

Boskov's team were a great attacking side but had a reputation for leaking goals at the other end, and that accounted for their fifth place finish in the league in 1988–89 as Giovanni Trapattoni's Inter stormed to the title. Still, the Sampdoria fans had the excitement of two cup finals to look forward to, as Mancini had scored twice in the second leg of the Coppa Italia semi-final, Atalanta being dismissed 6–3 on aggregate.

Before the June showpiece brought the Italian domestic season to an end, Samp had a trip to Berne in Switzerland to take on Barcelona in the Cup Winners' Cup final. Johan Cruyff's side were not the dominant force they were to become 20 years later, but were still packed with stars and led by England ace Gary Lineker and towering Spain striker Julio Salinas. In Berne's Wankdorf Stadium, they had too much know-how for an over-awed Samp, who were hit by the suspensions of Vierchowod and left back Amadeo Carboni , and had Vialli, stalwart full back Moreno Mannini and Luca Pellegrini all playing with injuries. Goals from Salinas and Luis Lopez settled the matter in Barca's favour, and Mancini missed Samp's best chances. But there was a feeling that this was only the beginning, and that Samp could go on to great things – if only their players could resist the tempting offers of bigger clubs.

With Juventus and AC Milan sniffing around, dangling lucrative contracts and the promise of glory, the senior stars got together for a dinner in 1989 to make a "blood pact". Seven key players in the Samp team already used to hang around together on a regular basis, and called themselves the Seven Dwarves. Mancini, nicknamed Cucciolo – the Italian equivalent of Dopey in the Walt Disney film – was the undoubted leader of the team by this point. He was sometimes allowed to take the half-time team talk by Boskov, attended board meetings and was even said to have input into the design of the kit. At the fateful dinner, he urged the players, one at a time, to stand and make a vow that they would not leave the club until they had won the Scudetto. His transformation was complete – for many years he had hankered after a move to his boyhood team Juventus, but now he was a Sampdoria man, through and through.

The Samp team celebrated their vow by retaining the Coppa Italia the following month. It was a tough ask against Napoli, who had finished runners-up in Serie A, in the two-legged final. The first game was in the Stadio San Paolo, the most hostile of all Italian stadiums, where the noise is skull-splitting, the ground lit by flares and crackling with animosity. Napoli were fresh from victory in the Uefa Cup final and, driven on by South American pair Maradona and Careca, took a slender first-leg lead, courtesy of a header from former Samp defender Alessandro Renica.

The return leg, on June 28, 1989, had to be played at Cremona, as Marassi was being rebuilt in readiness for the World Cup finals the following summer. The Samp team holed up in the spa town of Salsomaggiore Terme to prepare for the game – and their secluded concentration paid off. After his leadership off the field, Mancini showed he had the same quality on the field, having a hand in goals by Vialli, Cerezo and Vierchowod before earning and scoring a penalty for an emphatic 4–0 lead. The cup was in the bag, and the celebrating crowd were revelling in the beauty of Mancini's football. Now they were about to see the beast raging within.

Napoli turned ugly first, Alessandro Renica being dismissed for successive yellow cards. That set the tone for a fractious finish and a mass brawl. When the smoke had cleared, Sampdoria's masseur was also sent off, quickly followed by Mancini. It was an inauspicious end to another good season for the player and the club.

Another cup was in the bag, but the vow of those players who made the blood pact was yet to be made good, and with more foreign stars pouring into Serie A every season, there was danger that their dream would drown in a sea of expensive foreign imports. Boskov and Borea had other ideas – they knew they were just two or three players away from having a squad capable of challenging champions Inter, Maradona's Napoli, and the Milan of Gullit, van Basten and Frank Rijkaard who had just won the European Cup.

In the summer of 1989 they brought in midfielder Giovanni Invernizzi from relegated Como, Slovenian tough guy Srecko Katanec from Stuttgart and a dynamic, prematurely balding winger called Attilio Lombardo, who Mancini had spotted playing for Cremonese. For once, Mancini out-scored his partner Vialli, with 11 Serie A goals to his pal's ten, but still Samp could not break into the top four, as Napoli won the Scudetto. However, Samp did sample European glory for the first time, winning the Cup Winners' Cup with victory over Anderlecht in Gothenburg, where it was Vialli who stole the show.

After Sampdoria had breezed past Norwegian side Brann Bergen in the first round, Mancini earned his side a draw at Borussia

Dortmund, quick to spot the opportunity and calm enough to lob the keeper. The second leg was a formality as Vialli struck twice to put Samp in the quarter-finals.

Next up were Grasshopper of Switzerland, and Mancini planted a free kick on Vierchowod's head to put them ahead and then delivered a delicate side-foot volleyed cross for defender Urs Meier's diving own goal to make the first leg 2–0. Mancini's excellence at set-pieces made the second leg in Zurich a formality, arcing the ball onto Cerezo's head from a free kick. Grasshopper hit back to equalize, but a Mancini counter-attack teed up Lombardo to make it 2–1 on the night and 4–1 on aggregate.

The semi-final saw Samp up against Arsène Wenger's Monaco side, led by African Footballer of the Year George Weah. It was almost a derby match for Samp, with Monaco just a couple of hours' drive along the Mediterranean coast. Vialli scored twice in the away leg, the second from another pinpoint Mancini cross to make it 2–2 on the night, and goals from Vierchowod and Lombardo sealed a place in the final, to be held at the Nya Ullevi stadium in the Swedish city of Gothenburg on May 9, 1990. Opponents Anderlecht were in their second final in three seasons and had shown their mettle by knocking out holders Barcelona in the second round in front of 105,000 fans at the Camp Nou.

After 90 minutes of stalemate, with Mancini having one effort cleared off the line, Samp struck in extra time. Mancini burst into the area, and when he was tackled the ball fell for substitute Salsano. His shot was turned onto the post by keeper Filip de Wilde, and when the keeper failed to hold the rebound, Vialli pounced to run the ball into the net. The goal that sealed the 2–0 win was created by City's modern-day coaching triumvirate. The fresh legs of sub

Lombardo drove Samp forward, he fed Salsano, and the little schemer picked out Mancini, who had typically drifted wide. His cross meant Vialli could not miss, and the cup belonged to the Blucerchiati.

The 7,000 Samp fans in the 20,103 crowd at the Ullevi went wild, and the streets of Genoa were packed with fans, many wearing T-shirts depicting the "Goal Twins", Vialli and Mancini. As the team clambered down the steps of the plane at Genoa Airport, captain Luca Pellegrini hoisting the trophy aloft, those supporters were still in dreamland.

But for Mancini and the rest of the Seven Dwarves, it was still only a beginning. They had finished the league season in fifth place, and were in danger of being written off as merely a cup team, stylish enough to win trophies but lacking the substance to challenge for the Scudetto. Their defence of the Coppa Italia had not gone beyond the quarter-final stage, where they lost out to Juventus in a round-robin group which also included Pescara.

They would find the edge they needed in the anger and frustration created just weeks later by the "snub" delivered to the Sampdoria club in the World Cup finals.

Chapter Three
Forza Sampdoria

When Roberto Mancini became Manchester City manager in 2009, there were more than a few Blues fans who were asking "Roberto Who?"

Cosmopolitan English fans knew of the talented, maverick player who had lit up Serie A, but he was far from being a household name in England. The simple reason was that, apart from one Cup Winners' Cup triumph, a losing European Cup final appearance at Wembley and a brief dalliance with the 1988 European Championships, Mancini's talents never found the international stage they deserved.

Italian football fans revered him as a great, or despised him as a brat – or even both – but they all recognized him as a special talent. When it came to the national team, his stubbornness, and the short-sightedness of successive national team coaches, as well as the fact that his career coincided with those of team-mate Vialli and another great talent, Roberto Baggio, meant he played just 36 games for Italy, scoring four goals.

Mancini's international career was cursed from the start, as he ran into disciplinary trouble with national team coach Enzo Bearzot right from the off, killing his chances of playing in the 1986 World Cup finals. Mancini had been a fixture in the under-21 side from the age of 17, and captained them to the final of the European

Championships in 1986, where they lost to Spain on penalties in Valladolid. But an incident during Italy's close-season tour of North America in the summer of 1984 put his senior international career on hold.

The 19-year-old made his international debut by playing 45 minutes against Canada and then doing the same against the USA in New York four days later. After the second game, he headed into the Big Apple with experienced team-mates Claudio Gentile and Marco Tardelli to sample the delights of the trendy Studio 54 club – and he was the one caught by Bearzot, slipping back into the team hotel, after curfew. "He was waiting for me by the door when I got back a little late," said Mancini. "He insulted me with all the words under the sun. I should have apologized, that night or once we were back in Italy. That's what caused me to miss my second World Cup. New York was beautiful, full of lights, a paradise for me, not 20 years old. I did nothing wrong, just went back a little later than expected."

The story is redolent of Mancini's own time as a manager, when he had to discipline and forgive Mario Balotelli for a curfew transgression, and then made it plain that the errant Carlos Tevez was a simple apology away from being allowed back into the fold.

Bearzot was in no mood for forgiveness. He had recognized Mancini's talent from an early age – indeed he had included the 17-year-old in his provisional squad for the 1982 World Cup, but left him out of the final 22. The day after the player's curfew break, the two men argued again, with Mancini feeling aggrieved that the two older players had not also been punished, and Bearzot vowing that he would not play for him again.

The coach was as good as his word, and Mancini did not play for his country for the two years he remained in charge. Under Bearzot's stewardship, however, Italy had failed to qualify for Euro 1984 and then lost to France in the last 16 of the 1986 World Cup finals. When he resigned from his post, the coast was clear for Mancini. Azeglio Vicini got the job and Mancini was back in favour, as he had been captain of Vicini's under-21 squad.

Vicini's task was to phase out the national heroes who had won the World Cup in 1982, and re-model the national team around a new "golden generation" – principally Mancini, Vialli, goalkeeper Walter Zenga, defenders Franco Baresi and Paolo Maldini, and midfielders Carlo Ancelotti, Giuseppe Giannini and Roberto Donadoni. Mancini's rehabilitation in the national team began in Vicini's first game in charge, a friendly against Greece, fittingly held in Bologna, in October 1986, when he came on as a second-half substitute.

But more trouble was just around the corner, and it was again caused by Mancini's hot temper and outspoken nature. In the wake of the Totonero match-fixing scandal in 1986, the Italian Football Federation commissioner Franco Carraro had introduced new rules aimed at tightening up the system and ensuring wrongdoers were properly punished. One new rule was that no player who was serving a suspension could be picked for the national team. In January 1987, the 23-year-old Mancini put that to the test.

Samp lost a tight, tense match 1–0 at Atalanta to a controversial penalty. Samp defender Pietro Vierchowod seemed to accidentally collide with Atalanta's Cesare Prandelli after clearing the ball. Prandelli went down, and referee Alberto Boschi gave the penalty which won the game. It was the last in a line of questionable decisions which had gone against Sampdoria. Mancini was incensed, and didn't hold back when speaking to journalists after the game.

"The fans should stop beating each other up and invade the field to beat the referee," he said. "Boschi has targeted 11 players in white jerseys. He is a referee less than mediocre. Good for the third division, maybe – no, not even that, but only for matches between bachelors and married men. And what were his linesmen doing? You could have put any two people there."

He quickly retracted from his words, blaming the heat of the moment, and the fact that as someone who lived for football, he found defeat – and especially unjust defeat – hard to take. In a repentant statement, he harked back to his days as a kid at Bologna: "Football does not give you time to breathe. We had one or two training sessions a day, then eating, sleeping, training, never time to think or live like others of your age. And every day you are thinking of your game, the game you cannot lose. Then you lose in that way, and for once my life explodes."

It did explode, as ref Boschi asked the federation for permission to sue him for his comments. Vicini had already included Mancini in the squad for the Euro 88 qualifier against Malta the following week, but left him out of the match and out of the following qualifier in Portugal after he had been handed a three-match ban and a £1,100 fine for his outburst. Mancini did not play for his country again until he appeared as a substitute in the friendly draw with West Germany three months later, and that summer missed a penalty as Italy lost a Euro qualifier 1–0 to Sweden in Stockholm.

By the time Euro 1988 came around, however, Vialli and Mancini were Vicini's first-choice attackers. They were also wanted men, with Serie A's big clubs enviously eyeing the Goal Twins who were lighting up the relative football backwater of Genoa. Mancini won the Golden Guerin for 1987–88, an award given out by an Italian football magazine to the player with the best average rating from the three main sports newspapers.

The feisty young star was in the mood to show the rest of Europe what they had been missing, and was given the perfect stage to do so when Italy were drawn to contest the showpiece opening match of the tournament, against hosts West Germany, in Dusseldorf. He duly swept in the opening goal of the tournament, and then set off on a sprint for the touchline in an angry, ecstatic goal celebration aimed at his critics in the press box.

It was his first goal for his country, at the age of 23, and it looked like the launch of a new international star. As it turned out, it was his only goal at a major tournament. Italy reached the semi-finals with group wins over Spain and Denmark, but lost to the USSR – and that was the end of Mancini's stay on the big stage for his country, as he and Vialli were widely criticized.

He also suffered a loss of form heading into the 1990 World Cup, and found himself sitting on the bench for the entire tournament. Mancini had missed out by being too young in 1982, arguing with the coach in 1986, being out of form in 1990, and again arguing with the boss, this time Arrigo Sacchi, in 1994. It remains a matter of regret to Mancini, especially the frustration of 1990 when, aged 25, he should have been at the height of his powers and had the chance to strut his stuff on home soil, in a team among the favourites to lift the trophy.

Italy got as far as the semi-finals, thanks to the emergence of Salvatore "Toto" Schillaci, who came from nowhere to win the tournament's Golden Boot with six goals. He made his debut in Italy's first game, scoring the winner against Austria, and kept his place, while Vialli, perhaps suffering from not playing alongside his trusty partner Mancini, also lost form and was replaced by the rookie 23-year-old Baggio.

That places Mancini on an unenvied list of footballers, as one of the best never to have played at a World Cup, alongside stars like George Best, Ryan Giggs, Jari Litmanen, George Weah and Alfredo di Stefano. The difference between Mancini and those others, however, is that the misfortunes of Best, Giggs, Litmanen and Weah were the consequence of playing for small countries, Northern Ireland, Wales, Finland and Liberia respectively, while Real Madrid legend di Stefano paid for changing nationality from Argentinian to Spanish, and was then injured.

Vicini had predicted that Mancini could be one of the surprises of Italia 90, which later brought a sardonic response from the player: "The surprise was that I never got to play! I wasted 70 days of my life between the training camp and the World Cup and didn't get a single minute. Seventy days! Seventy days I'll never get back."

Mancini was especially frustrated that Vicini and his successor Sacchi did not feel Mancini could play with Baggio – it had to be one or the other. He also felt he and his Sampdoria team-mates were the victims of the widely suspected bias towards the giant clubs Juventus and AC Milan. Keeper Gianluca Pagliuca also did not play, Vialli was hastily dropped, and defender Pietro Vierchowod only took part in the third place play-off.

Mancini criticized Vicini for his tactics, and blamed him for their semi-final exit to Argentina. He said the quick, tough Vierchowod, who sat alongside him on the bench, should have been detailed to mark Diego Maradona. "He would have been cancelled out, and everything would have changed," Mancini later said. "Even a blind man would have seen it, but unfortunately not Vicini."

His suspicions, that the big clubs wielded too much power, and that the smaller clubs were fighting an unjust system, were to be vindicated by the Calciopoli scandal six years later. Mancini said of his stunted international career: "It was my fault. My fault that I played for Samp. Just as it was Vialli's fault and Pietro Vierchowod's fault that they were also with Samp and not with a 'big club'."

That suspicion about favouritism offered to the established big clubs has spilled over into his City career, bringing from him dark hints that some clubs are treated differently by referees and the football authorities. Such comments are marked down as "mind games" but are more likely a hangover from Mancio's more fiery days when he found it hard to bite his lip, and was seething with a sense of injustice, both real and imagined.

The whole Sampdoria club felt affronted by the snubs to Mancini, Pagliuca, Vialli and Vierchowod. The sweetness of the Cup Winners' Cup triumph – and for Mancini even the personal happiness of marrying Neapolitan lawyer Federica Morelli – was soured when the players were denied the chance to shine on home soil. However, the disappointment of 1990 did have one galvanizing effect: their determined anger led them to their only league title.

No-one really gave Sampdoria much of a chance as they headed into the 1990–91 season. The dismal form of Vialli at Italia 90, and the fact that Mancini and Pagliuca had fidgeted on the bench for the entire tournament, reinforced that prediction. The World Cup final, held in Rome, appeared to be a pointer to the destiny of the following season's Serie A, with frustrated losing finalist Maradona ready to inspire Napoli to the title for the third time, while victorious German trio Andreas Brehme, Lothar Matthaus and Jurgen Klinsmann were key men in the Inter team.

The trouble was that no-one had handed Sampdoria a script, and the fact that their stars had such a nightmarish World Cup only served to strengthen and inspire them. Borea had again gone to work in the summer, not shopping in the inflated marketplace of the finals, but instead picking up Dynamo Kiev midfielder Alexei Mikhailichenko, Ivano Bonetti from Bologna and striker Marco Branca from Udinese, giving Mancini fresh hope that he might finally play as a midfielder. Mancini had always been a better creator of goals than finisher, and felt his game suffered whenever he was asked to play up front. At times, he cursed the nine goals he scored as a teenager in the struggling Bologna team, as they appeared to have tattooed him for life as a front man. He was happier supplying the ammunition for the deadly Vialli, or swinging in corners and free kicks for the power of centre back Vierchowod.

With the World Cup over, the season of destiny had arrived. To get a sense of Sampdoria in 1991, think Manchester City in 2012, and double it. The wait for City fans had been excruciating – any Blue under 50 could not remember their last league title win, back in 1968. But Samp had never won the title, and with the wealth and power of Juventus, Inter, AC Milan and Roma arrayed against them, it felt as though they never would.

But Mancini and Vialli led a team bonded by a loyalty to each other and to the cause, and which now had defensive security to add to its attacking beauty. Even with Vialli injured, they were unbeaten for the first nine games and hit top spot on October 28, 1990 in style, going to Milan and winning 1–0 against van Basten, Gullit and Co. An astonishing 4–1 win in the Napoli cauldron had the critics taking notice, with Mancini and Vialli scoring two apiece.

The fourth Samp goal, in the final minute, is one of the great Serie A goals – Lombardo broke down the right, and his cross was slightly behind Mancio, who was sprinting at top speed into the left-hand side of the box. Without checking his stride, he showed incredible balance and technique to reach back with his right foot and smash a volley past goalkeeper Giovanni Galli.

Just as Mancini's City were to do 21 years later, Mancini's Sampdoria found their fires dampened by the rains of winter. They suffered their first defeat at home to Genoa, in the Lighthouse Derby, named after the beacon tower which serves as a symbol for the city. But their rivals were looking less than convincing, and when joint leaders Inter visited Marassi in December, two Vialli goals and Mancini's sweet volley secured the two points. The fervour was soon dampened as defeats by Torino and Lecce saw Samp in familiar territory, sitting behind Milan, Inter and Juve, three clubs who between them had won 38 of the previous 59 Serie A titles. But Samp put on another winning spurt, notching up five victories on the trot, Mancini earning a penalty against Juve which Vialli dispatched, and then pulling off an acrobatic diving header in the last minute to beat Parma 1–0.

Samp were now in full flow and when they faced Milan, Mancini was inspired. An outrageous lob over the heads of Paolo Maldini and Franco Baresi – arguably the two finest Italian defenders in history – coaxed a penalty which again Vialli netted, and then Mancini secured both points with a delicate second goal.

This was followed by a 4–1 home win over Napoli, remembered chiefly as being Maradona's last game in Serie A after he tested positive for cocaine. Coupled with Inter's defeat in the Milan derby, it meant Samp had a three-point lead with eight games to go. The distraction of defending their Cup Winners' Cup, meanwhile, was removed by a quarter-final defeat by Legia Warsaw.

Since Christmas, Boskov had been pointing to the San Siro showdown with Inter on May 5 as a possible title decider, just as years later Mancini would flag up the Manchester derby, three games from the end of the 2011–12 season, as the crunch match. As if to crank up the tension for that game, Serie A took a fortnight's international break, but that gave Mancini and Vialli a timely boost, as they were picked together for their country for the first time in over 16 months. Mancini had said that he was beginning to feel his international career was over, at the age of 26, but the remarkable form of the Goal Twins finally broke the stranglehold of Baggio and Schillaci. In the game Mancini picked up a foot wound requiring two stitches, but that was not going to keep him out of the meeting with Inter.

Inter needed to win, Sampdoria to avoid defeat, hardly the recipe for a classic. But what a game it was! Klinsmann, Matthaus and Co. hammered away at the stubborn Samp defence, which was backed up by a brilliant display in goal by Pagliuca – who saved a Matthaus penalty – and helped by some poor finishing and a couple of curious decisions by the officials. Mancini's afternoon was short-lived as he went nose to nose with Giuseppe Bergomi after the Inter defender accused him of diving. It was a minor confrontation but the referee over-reacted by showing both men a red card, and as they walked off together in mutual sympathy, Bergomi was hit by objects thrown by his own supporters as they targeted Mancini. Pagliuca was hit by an umbrella, fans fought in the stands and smoke canisters were thrown, amid chaotic scenes which would earn Inter a one-match ground closure.

Mancini could only watch with mixed feelings from the sidelines as Dossena crashed in his first goal of the season and Vialli rounded keeper Walter Zenga to make it 2–0, and celebrated with a somersault. It was a game that had everything – seasoned commentator Martin Tyler said on air: "In years to come, people will be saying, 'I was there. I was at that game'." It meant everything to Samp, who were four points clear of second-placed Milan, in the days of two points for a win. Now it was a case of holding their nerve, but again fate had dealt Mancini a cruel blow.

For the confrontation between Mancini and Bergomi, both men received two-match bans, and that meant Samp had to try to win the title without the man who had proved their main creative force all season. The team, and the club, were in unknown territory. They had never finished higher than fourth in their history, and needed three points from three games, two of them without Mancini. Genoa were good neighbours, knocking Inter out of the race with a 3–0 win, while Invernizzi's goal earned Samp a draw at Torino which kept them ahead of Milan. The stage was set at Marassi on May 19, 1991, with lowly Lecce the visitors and two points needed.

Mancini was still suspended, having had an appeal turned down, so he was a spectator on the day the blood pact came to fulfilment. Within half an hour Samp were 3–0 up, courtesy of Cerezo, Moreno Mannini's stunning volley and the inevitable Vialli goal, and coasted to the title. The best team in Serie A had won the title, and done it with flair, and their star, Mancini, had won his second Golden Guerin as Serie A's most consistent player. European Football Yearbook described Samp as "far and away the classiest act in the league". But Samp were also known for their sense of fun – for the final match, which ended 3–3 at Lazio, the entire squad bleached their hair, much to the harrumphing dismay of Italian traditionalists. Mancini bagged a goal, his 12th of the season, in that meaningless last game – not bad for someone who still grumbled that he wasn't a striker. Then it was back to Genoa for the biggest party in the city's history. Mancini wanted something as a permanent reminder of that remarkable season, and had the Samp symbol, of an old sailor smoking a pipe, tattooed above his right ankle.

Dreams of a league and cup double fell apart as Samp were beaten in the Coppa Italia final over two legs by Roma, but that seemed to emphasize the fact that the "cup team" had matured into true champions, and a club with real European stature. Once the euphoria had died down, the Sampdoria blood brothers had one more task facing them, their first European Cup campaign.

The problem was that the pact they had made had come to fulfilment – the title had been won, and it felt too much like an end, rather than a beginning. In 1991–92, Samp found themselves struggling in the league, before a rally saw them finish in sixth place. But they had other fish to fry, and a bold run to the final in their first European Cup campaign more than sated supporters who were concerned about the feeble defence of the Scudetto.

Mancini was suspended for Sampdoria's historic first European Cup tie, but not needed as Rosenborg were seen off 5–0 at Marassi. He then sealed a 2–1 win in the return leg with a last-minute penalty. Hungarian side Honved were dispatched in the second round, pitching Sampdoria into one of two four-team groups, of which the winners would meet in the final. A win over Red Star Belgrade, and a goalless draw with Panathinaikos in Greece, with Mancini injured, got them off to a good start, but then Samp lost 3–2 in Belgium to erstwhile European foes Anderlecht. The Belgians were beaten in the return at Marassi, with Mancini scoring again, and Samp made themselves favourites to reach the final when they beat Red Star 3–1 in the away fixture. The game was held in Sofia, Bulgaria, due to Yugoslavia's slide into civil war, and in a hostile atmosphere Mancini secured victory with an important third goal.

Now Samp needed a draw at home to Panathinaikos, unless Red Star could win by six goals at Anderlecht. The Greeks stunned Marassi by scoring first, but a moment of Mancini magic, with instant thigh control and a crashing finish from a difficult angle, sent Samp to the final, to be held at Wembley Stadium, against Barcelona, on May 20, 1992. That night was to signal the end of Samp's golden era. Boskov had already hinted that he would leave at the end of the season, and strong rumours were sweeping the Samp camp in the build-up to the final that Vialli would also be going, to seek greater fame and fortune at Juventus.

The final was an inglorious end to a great Sampdoria career for Vialli, who tried too hard to go out on a high and missed three good chances. Against a Barca side packed with the quality of Dutch ace Ronald Koeman, Danish genius Michael Laudrup and brilliant Bulgarian Hristo Stoichkov, such profligacy was bound to get punished. Koeman delivered the blow in extra time, hammering in an unstoppable shot from a free kick routine, although Samp furiously argued that it had not been a free kick in the first place. Indeed, Mancini was booked for a prolonged moan at referee Aron Schmidhuber, and later picked up a four-match ban for something he said to the official after the game.

Mancini walked off the Wembley pitch in tears, not to return to the stadium until he led his Manchester City team out for the 2011 FA Cup semi-final against Manchester United – a far happier affair for him. On that disappointing May night in 1992, things looked bad for Mancini as the team he had helped to put together, and weld into a fearsome, swashbuckling side, was about to lose its coach, its top goalscorer Vialli, and its midfield driving force Cerezo, who retired.

Boskov was replaced by a bookish, bespectacled Swede named Sven-Goran Eriksson, who had made his name in Italy as a thoughtful coach at Roma and Fiorentina before leading Benfica to three league titles, two European finals and a Portuguese Cup. His appointment would delay the inevitable Sampdoria slump and bring them one more trophy, and a few more glory days at Marassi, before he and Mancini left, and the club sank back into the morass of Italian football.

Eriksson had flown to neutral territory for the job interview, meeting Mantovani in the Sampdoria owner's sumptuous Monte Carlo hotel suite. When he walked into the room, he was amazed to see Mancini and Vialli sitting alongside the president – it was an early indicator of the power they held, although by the time he took up the post, Vialli had departed for Juventus.

The unusual job interview was the start of a nine-year relationship which was to set Mancini on his way to a successful career in management, helping to turn the impetuous, headstrong player into a mature, measured coach, without losing any of his legendary fire. Eriksson would also provide Mancini with his first links to Manchester City, as the Swede took Mancini's son Filippo on loan when he was in charge of the Blues in 2008.

It was an unlikely combination. The coach was quietly spoken, with a gentle manner. Some critics half expected that the fiery Mancini would eat him alive, or at least make his life a misery by colluding with Mantovani. It was a false assessment, as Eriksson's serene exterior belies inner steel and a sharp mind, and Mancini's clashes with previous coaches had been born out of a desire to better himself and his team, rather than any self-interest.

Boskov had learned how to tap into that passion, to use president Mantovani as an outlet for the player's frustration, and to get Mancini involved as a team leader and later captain. Eriksson knew exactly what he was taking on – he had watched from the stands at Wembley as Sampdoria lost the European Cup final to Barcelona, and Mancini had talked himself into trouble with the authorities. Eriksson later admitted that he had wondered what he had let himself in for, saying: "As a person everybody loves Mancini, but with referees? Oooof. He was awful. He couldn't control himself."

It was an aspect of Mancini's personality that Eriksson could not contain, but the fire and the spirit which engendered that flaw would serve him well, and the coach realized very early in their relationship that Mancini would be his on-field general. Mancini's position at Samp was unquestionably powerful – the story goes that Mantovani would ring up Eriksson to ask if Mancio was playing, and would only turn up to watch if the answer was in the affirmative!

Eriksson had a host of new players with which to begin his rebuilding of the team in the 1992–93 season. The sale of Vialli to Juve had provided funds by bringing in a world record fee of £12 million, and in came England defender Des Walker from Nottingham Forest, Vladimir Jugovic from Red Star Belgrade, Enrico Chiesa from Chieti, and Michele Serena from Verona. Clearly it was going to be a season of transition, but it was still an inauspicious start for Eriksson as Sampdoria crashed out of the Coppa Italia to Serie B side Cesena.

With Vialli gone, the goalscoring burden fell on Mancini, and he came up with a goal per game at the beginning of the season – before again falling foul of an irate referee in the third league game, at Udinese. The trouble arose when Mancini was having his shirt pulled by Udinese defender Renzo Contratto, and referee Walter Cinciripini warned him that if he continued, he would whistle for a penalty. When the two clashed again and he heard a whistle, Mancini thought he had a spot kick, but the referee had penalized him for diving. Mancini walked over to the bench and told Eriksson to substitute him before he was sent off – and was promptly shown a red card, the referee believing he had said something insulting. Mancini was later accused of telling Cinciripini that he was heading for the press room, to verbally slaughter him, which he denied. The authorities believed the ref, and the player got a three-match ban and a fine despite his protestations of innocence.

His 40-day absence was made more painful by the fact that, without him, Sampdoria's promising start petered out. Mancini returned to inspire a 4–1 derby win over Genoa, but Eriksson's first season meandered to a close. They clearly needed reinforcements, and Mancini sought out Mantovani, urging him to bolster the flagging team. Sampdoria's dream was fading, and Mantovani himself was dying, succumbing to health problems which had dogged him for years. The president's last wish was to provide the supporters, and his loyal players, with a new team. In came David Platt from Juventus for £5.2 million and the great Ruud Gullit for a bargain £500,000 from Milan, while Fausto Salsano returned after three years at Roma.

Mancini had been pursuing Platt for three years, ever since he watched him star for England at Italia 90. In fact, Vialli had tried to persuade the Oldham-born Platt to join them in Genoa after the third place play-off, in which Italy beat England. The following summer, Bari beat Sampdoria to the punch, paying a British record £5.5 million, but it soon became apparent that Platt was destined for a bigger club, and before long Juventus were on his trail. When Bari played at Marassi, and the players lined up in the tunnel, Platt later recalled that he could feel Mancini's eyes boring into him. As they walked out on to the pitch, Mancio asked the Englishman whether he was staying at Bari or going to Juve, and when Platt answered that he was undecided, Mancini asked him, there and then, to join him at Samp.

They agreed to talk after the game, but fate intervened as after just nine minutes Platt was taken to hospital for X-rays on an ankle injury. He limped back into the stadium five minutes before the end of the match, only to discover that Mancio had also damaged an ankle and been taken to the same hospital! Mancini rang Platt a few weeks later, again urging him to join Samp and letting him in on the secret that his England team-mate Walker was already on his way to Marassi that summer.

When Platt got another call, from Mancini's "twin" Vialli, he thought it was another attempt to lure him to Sampdoria, but it was quite the opposite. Vialli was on the verge of leaving to join Juve, and wanted Platt to join him there. That clinched it for Platt, as he believed that Vialli would prove to be a hit at the Stadio delle Alpi, and that his departure would significantly weaken Sampdoria. Six months after his £6.5 million move, Platt regretted his choice, as he found himself the odd man out in a team which had four overseas players – German pair Jurgen Kohler and Andreas Moller, Platt and Brazilian Julio Cesar – in a league with a three-foreigner rule.

Sampdoria, and Mancini, finally got their man in the summer of 1993, the £5.2 million fee making Platt the most costly footballer in history with combined fees of £17.4 million. When he reported to the team hotel for pre-season training, Mancini made Platt his room-mate, beginning a friendship which remains close.

The arrivals of Platt and Gullit were momentous for Mancini, who saw fresh hope for the future, and they were also good business by Mantovani, who actually turned a profit by selling Marco Lanna to Roma and sending the disappointing Walker to Sheffield Wednesday after one season. Gullit was a true world star, having won two European Cups and three Scudetti with Milan, but he had been marginalized at the San Siro, and the story doing the rounds was that his knees had gone. Gullit knew that was not the case, but Samp were still taking a gamble, even for half a million pounds.

Samp were back in business, and Platt soon had Mancini marked down as a "genius". As he wrote in his autobiography, "Mancini could put the ball where he wanted, whenever he wanted." But Mancini's eternal problem remained: now not only was he still being forced to play as a striker, he had a new partner, in Gullit, who also preferred to play in a withdrawn role – and it worked like a dream. Platt and Gullit scored on their league debuts for Samp, and by October the side were sharing top spot with Milan and Parma.

Some felt that Mancini might be jealous of a major star like Gullit walking into a team where he was very much the number one, a claim which exasperated Eriksson, who said: "Mancini is not a player, he is a Sampdoria fan. He reasons with his heart and rejoices at the team's success. It was he who asked Mantovani to get Gullit! Mancini is smart and knows the Dutchman can bring us a major championship."

It was fitting that the new, attacking Sampdoria should put on a show to win 4–1 at Atalanta on October 3, with two goals from Gullit and one each from Mancini and Platt. It was the last game before the death of Mantovani. The passing of his football "father", at the age of 62, was a bitter blow to Mancini. His reverence for the man was illustrated in 2011 when, asked which three people, living or dead, he would invite to a special dinner, he answered: "The Pope, Paolo Mantovani and Sheikh Mansour."

Vialli and Cerezo had left, and now the man whose love, money and vision had created something beautiful at a provincial football backwater, was also gone. Mancini and Sampdoria would never be the same again. "The saddest day of my life" was how Mancini described the day of Mantovani's death, but he added, "I am sure what he has built will not be lost." Along with five others from the Scudetto-winning team, Mancini carried the coffin on Mantovani's final journey, and the golden era was truly at an end, even if there was to be a sweet swansong at the end of the season.

Mancini urged Mantovani's family to continue his good work, and even hinted that he would like to stay at Samp for life, causing some to earmark him as a future sporting director. But within two months Mantovani's son Enrico had been installed as president, and the relationship between Mancio and the son of his mentor was to end badly.

Genoese grief was eased by the return of Samp's attacking flair, with Gullit, Mancini and Platt scoring 36 Serie A goals between them and taking them to third place in the table. They had chased Milan throughout the season, and ended the Rossoneri's amazing 72-week stay at the top of Serie A by coming from 2–0 down to win 3–2, Gullit scoring the winner against his former club. That was one of 15 goals in 31 Serie A games for the reborn Gullit, and he also played a part in the march to the Coppa Italia final. Penalty shoot-out wins over Pisa and Roma were followed by a victory over Inter before Platt's great overhead kick helped them to a semi-final win over Parma.

The opposition in the final was Serie B outfit Ancona, who had knocked out Napoli and Torino along the way. They held Samp 0–0 in the first leg, and Mancini was injured for the second leg which meant he missed yet another big occasion as six second-half goals gave his team a 6–1 triumph, and a return to European football. It was another trophy, on another bitter-sweet day for Mancini, but it was to be his last medal for Sampdoria. He would linger on for three more years before he realized that the dream truly was over, and there would be no revival.

Chapter Four
From Rome to Leicester

When the news broke that Roberto Mancini was ready to leave Sampdoria, the supporters were furious. They marched on his house in a bid to talk him around, and told club president Enrico Mantovani that he would have his legs broken if he allowed it to happen. Mancini's team-mate David Platt would later recall those tempestuous days with a grin: "I remember when a crowd gathered outside Wayne Rooney's house, because they thought he was leaving. There must have been about 50. When Robbie was at Sampdoria and he said he might go to Inter Milan, a crowd of 10,000 gathered outside his house, all begging him to stay." That was in the autumn of 1996, and Mancini's days at Sampdoria were heading to a close.

Mancini's troubled international career had already fizzled to an ignoble end, six years after his Italia 90 snub. After all the misunderstandings with successive coaches, and the failure of the national team to release and utilize his talents, Mancio finally called it a day, at the age of 29. After his disagreements with Vicini, Mancini had been tentatively reintroduced into the national squad. He had been a difficult player to ignore, as he drove Sampdoria to glory in Serie A and Europe. The two men might have had their rows, but Vicini recognized that a talent like Mancio's could not be spurned, especially with Euro 92 qualifiers to be won.

The trouble was that Mancini played in most of those qualifiers, and Italy flopped, finishing behind the USSR in their group and missing out on the tournament finals. Vicini paid the price, and in came Arrigo Sacchi, who had won two European Cups and a league title with AC Milan, and based his success on defensive security. He took a hard line with Mancini from the start, leaving him out of his first squad, claiming that the Sampdoria star wanted the national team to be built around him, "which is impossible," said Sacchi. What made this latest snub hard to take for Mancini was that Sacchi's first game in charge was on his home turf, in Genoa.

Sacchi told Mancini from the outset he would only be picked if Baggio was unavailable, and Mancini at least appreciated his honesty. A series of niggling injury problems also disrupted his international career, but in the immediate aftermath of the tearful European Cup final defeat in London, Mancini had the consolation of playing his first international for eight months, against Ireland during the Azzurri's summer tour of the USA.

Club and country provided a strange dual experience for Mancini. His club could barely function without him – one Italian newspaper declared that Sampdoria had an "addiction" to him – but his national team, or at least the men in charge, seemed to want to kick the habit. The ban for his verbal clash with referee Cinciripini, and injury, further hampered Mancini's attempts to impress Sacchi. He starred in a 6–1 home win over Malta, scoring twice, and Sacchi gave his own verdict on the mystery of Mancini as an international: "Roberto is a very sensitive boy who suffers a lot from the expectations of national public opinion. We need to leave him free to play without too much responsibility."

Mancini had considered quitting the national team out of respect for Sampdoria, who gave him the "tranquillity and continuity" he needed to flourish. But the concord with Sacchi had him once more hopeful of achieving international level. Once again, that hope was to be dashed. The debate had raged in Italian football circles about whether Baggio and Mancini could play in the same team, and the pair had only fleetingly disproved the critics, notably when two goals from the Divine Ponytail – as Baggio was to become known – and one from Mancini kept Italy on course for the 1994 World Cup finals in the USA with a 3–0 win in Estonia in September 1993.

That was a fleeting moment, and Mancini was soon back to the frustration of being behind Baggio in the pecking order, while being one of Serie A's brightest stars for Sampdoria. Part of the problem was that Mancini could not thrive under men like Vicini and Sacchi, who had strict ideas about the way the game should be played. Boskov and Eriksson allowed greater freedom of expression, and placed Mancini at the heart of what they did. When, after a poor Italian display against Germany, Mancio bore the brunt of the criticism for the defeat and calls were being made for an end to his international career, Eriksson eloquently defended his player. "I don't understand why so many people are damning Roberto," he said. "In Stuttgart the whole national team played badly, and was only saved by Pagliuca, so why ask for his head? Perhaps, in his heart, he will be happy if the coach does announce his retirement. It would be the end of a nightmare which started ten years ago in Canada, when Enzo Bearzot for the first time made him wear a shirt too plain to reflect the colours of his imagination."

Mancini himself had seen and heard enough, and after discussing the matter with Sacchi, was left out of the squad for the World Cup finals in 1994, which would have been his last chance to translate his genius into global stardom. At the age of 29, his international career – of 36 caps and four goals – was over. "After ten years of trying I realized I would never have broken through with the Azzurri," he said. "My fault was that I needed unconditional trust. I still regret not finding a coach who told me, 'You own the shirt for ten games.'"

Now he had to focus on his club football. Sampdoria had been Serie A's top scorers, and their fans delighted in being Italian football's great entertainers once again in 1994–95, but their defensive frailties stopped them from really challenging champions Milan. Gullit returned to Milan in the summer of 1994, and Pagliuca left too, in exchange for experienced international Walter Zenga, while Yugoslav set-piece genius Sinisa Mihajlovic also joined. Gullit was back at Samp by November, his last fling at Milan having lasted just a few months, but he appeared to have lost his motivation – and in a series of dressing-room confrontations with Mancini he was told as much, in no uncertain terms. Samp's famous team spirit had crumbled as Gullit and Mancini clashed, and their attacking flair was gone. Mancini ended the season as top scorer with 12 goals, but it was to be a frustrating season as the Blucerchiati finished eighth, their lowest placing for nearly a decade.

That disappointment was eased by a run to the Cup Winners' Cup semi-finals. Samp muddled through the first two rounds without Mancini, as he served a four-match ban, but he rescued his side in a quarter-final tie against Bobby Robson's Porto, who had a 1–0 lead from the first leg at Marassi. Mancini made up for time lost through his ban with a stunning volley to level in Portugal, and Samp held their nerve in the penalty shoot-out to set up a semi-final meeting with Arsenal.

This was a two-legged thriller which began in London with
unlikely Gunners hero Steve Bould scoring twice in two minutes.
Although Ian Wright added a third, Mancini, playing as a lone
striker, set up Jugovic for two goals and Samp went back to Italy
with a 3–2 deficit. Samp had been without the suspended Platt
and Mihajlovic, and had Gullit ineligible as he had already
played for Milan in European competition. But with Vierchowod
returning from injury and Mihajlovic back, Samp were confident
of success in the second leg. Mancini got the Blucerchiati off to
a great start by lobbing goalkeeper David Seaman, but Wright
equalized and, with ten minutes left, Arsenal seemed to be heading
into the final. Then 19-year-old striker Claudio Bellucci scored
twice to nudge Samp ahead, until Stefan Schwarz drilled in a low
free kick with two minutes on the clock. The tie went to penalties
and with Mancini and Platt in the tunnel unable to watch, Samp
ran into an inspired Seaman, who saved three of their five spot
kicks, and the Gunners were in the final, where they lost to
Real Zaragoza.

For a club of Sampdoria's size, no trophies and no European
place meant players had to be sold in the summer of 1995. Mancini
himself had a disappointing season, dogged by injury, poor form
and his rows with Gullit, and the side was weakened again by
the departure of Gullit to Chelsea and, more importantly, Platt's
departure for Arsenal in a £4.75 million deal, to be replaced by Ajax
midfielder Clarence Seedorf.

Lombardo, Vierchowod and Jugovic all went to Juventus, and
in came Christian Karembeu from Nantes, as well as Enrico Chiesa
for a third spell with the club. Samp were selling experience and
bringing in talented youth, and more than ever relied on Mancini as

the focal point of the team. Mantovani had declared Mancini to be "unsaleable" despite interest from all the big clubs.

That was some comfort for Eriksson, who had been told that Samp would have to sell every summer to survive while not in European competition. The coach later said of his star: "He can assess tactical changes during a match himself and has the ability to turn the game around. Your job as a coach is easy when players are so good tactically. It didn't hurt that he was also a footballing genius. He was a natural leader in a very characteristic sort of way."

The Swede was a huge influence on Mancini's own management style, especially his dedication to detail and the exhaustive work on team shape and tactics which would puzzle and exasperate some of his English players when Mancio first moved to Manchester. Eriksson also gave a glimpse of a side of Mancini's personality which has stood him in good stead, both as a player and coach, when he described him as one of those sportsmen who "have the will to win and, obviously, hate to lose. But they don't take defeat to heart and their anxiety is just as low when they turn up for the next match."

That was just as well, because 1995–96 was another tough season for Samp, again finishing eighth and taking an early tumble in the Coppa Italia, and that led to more frustration, and another clash with authority, for Mancini. In the goalless draw with Inter in November 1995, Mancini was booked for diving when he went down under a challenge from his old Samp team-mate and Inter goalkeeper Pagliuca. Incandescent with rage, Mancini marched over to the dugout, threw his captain's armband to the ground, removed his shin pads and demanded to be substituted, claiming he would never play again.

Eriksson refused his player's demand, and soon wished he had listened. Mancini's rage was unabated as he shouted something towards Enrico Mantovani in the stand, and then called referee Marcello Nicchi "a cheat". Pagliuca tried to lead his old team-mate away, fearing he would do something silly and end up with a life ban, but Mancio was red-carded and stormed away from the stadium before the end of the goalless draw. This took place in front of a delegation from Arsenal delegation, who were pondering a possible £5 million move for the player, and may well have helped them reach a decision.

Mancini was banned for six weeks and fined £3,800, a punishment which even shocked Eriksson: "It is like he has punched the referee or something," he said. But the coach also recognized the problem: "I hope this ban will make him understand you cannot fight against the referees, as they always have the last word. It is useless to try to change the world." Sampdoria were also punished, with a fine of £12,000, as referee Nicchi was hit by coins thrown by the fans, and his car was attacked as he left the stadium.

Paul Ince played in that match, shortly after his move from Manchester United, but he has more magical memories of taking on Mancini: "I was told to do a man-to-man job on him and the first couple of minutes I went down the back of his legs, which he wasn't too pleased about. But in the next 15 minutes he nutmegged me three or four times, so I went and marked someone else!"

Eriksson's quandary was clear, but he knew that being heavy-handed would do no good – the player was hard enough on himself. The coach said later: "If I had been a strict disciplinarian with Mancini, he would have been a poor player. He could find solutions on the field which you wouldn't find in any textbook."

Mancini searched his own soul for answers to his temperament, but found none: "Maybe it is because I am always at the centre of attention. I find it hard to control myself, so for years I did not speak after games, to avoid trouble."

Other clubs sensed that Mancini's time at Sampdoria was coming to an end. Mantovani had again "sold the family silver" in the summer of 1996, as Eriksson later put it, by accepting offers for Chiesa and Seedorf, although Mancini was mollified by the arrivals of Juan Sebastian Veron from Boca Juniors and striker Vincenzo Montella, who made the controversial move across the city from Genoa. Montella proved to be a big hit, scoring 22 goals and helping Mancini to 15, his best total for six years, and up until Christmas the Blucerchiati were in the title hunt, with Veron running midfield and Mihajlovic also to the fore.

But there was already dissent in the air. Eriksson's job came under threat after Genoa knocked Sampdoria out of the Coppa Italia, and in November, when Inter came calling, it appeared Mancini was finally on his way out of the club in a £4.2 million move. He had been spotted dining with Inter owner Massimo Moratti, and it was known that he was disillusioned with Samp's policy of selling their best players. He made no secret of his feelings: "I am no longer 25, I am nearly 32, and Sampdoria has no immediate future. We have good young players and I am happy to help them grow, but when they do, I will be too old to play with them." He also revealed for the first time an admiration for the English game, saying he had begun to find watching Italian football boring and that he found more excitement watching Barcelona, Brazilian star Ronaldo and "the spirit of the English, who are always trying to score".

Samp fans reacted furiously when Mancini hinted that the home game with Piacenza, in November 1996, might be his last for the Blucerchiati, after 14 glorious years. Mancini made it worse, scoring twice and setting up the other in a 3–0 win, and the fans pleaded with him to stay throughout the game, while again threatening to break the president's legs if he left. The shaken Mantovani decided to turn down the offer from Roy Hodgson's Inter and enforce the new five-year contract Mancini had signed just five months earlier. Mancini publicly said he was "deeply disappointed" but vowed to give his all for Sampdoria.

The passion to win was still there, as Veron – who went on to become a star with Mancini at Lazio and played for Manchester United and Chelsea – soon found out. The Argentine star took a poor corner kick in a game against Piacenza, and Mancini politely asked him to lift it higher the next time. Veron reacted with an insult, and that was a red rag to a Sampdoria bull. When Veron reached the dressing-room, he found Mancini stripped to the waist, wanting to fight him. "He is not an easy person, you know, he has this complicated personality," Veron was to say later. "Fortunately, there were some team-mates who didn't let him punch me. I knew that I had showed a bad attitude towards him on the field. So, when he had calmed, I apologized to him."

Despite his move to Inter falling through, Mancini still knew his days at Sampdoria were numbered, and would probably come to a close at the end of the season. That did not affect his commitment to the club's cause – in fact he scored the last-minute winner against Inter in the San Siro just a few weeks after the transfer was thwarted. Samp went on a great run, winning six and drawing one to sit two points behind leaders Juventus. Mancini was the inspiration

– Eriksson said he had "dragged us to unexpected levels" – with a series of great displays topped by a hat-trick in a remarkable 5–4 win at Udinese. But Eriksson himself had already decided to leave, lining up a move to join Blackburn Rovers at the end of the season, an agreement on which he eventually reneged in order to join Lazio instead. The announcement, in February, that the coach was leaving, caused a collapse in dressing-room morale at Samp, especially as it had already become clear that Mancini would probably go with him. They finished sixth, enough for a Uefa Cup place, and the Swede left for Lazio.

Mancini was more disappointed than most, saying of Eriksson: "I learned many things from him. Before he came, we played defensive, man-for-man football. He gave us our freedom. He likes to play with the ball on the floor, and he is never scared. His way is to attack and we did so, even at places like Milan and Juventus."

Soon afterwards Mancini followed Eriksson, his relationship with Enrico Mantovani now beyond repair. The president was not impressed, later saying: "Our relationship went into a crisis when I started to treat Mancini like an adult, after years of an exaggerated paternal relationship. Mancini is a spoiled boy who thinks the world owes him everything. He wanted to choose the players we signed, when the coaches wanted half a billion lire for them, and he wanted many other things that I was not capable of guaranteeing."

Finishing at Sampdoria was a heart-rending moment for Mancini, as he played his final game, against Fiorentina, after 15 years of service which has established him as the greatest player in their history. To rub salt in the wounds of the grieving fans, Mancini had just been named Italian footballer of the year. But his mind was made up, and he said ahead of his final game: "The choice was made a couple of months ago, at great cost, because this team is my life, and will be even after Sunday. I don't want to go into reasons, as I don't want any controversy. I will never forget Sampdoria. I may have won less than I possibly could, but the love is worth more than success. I have given so much, but I got even more back."

It had been a remarkable stay in Genoa, with 424 appearances and 132 goals, and Mancini had been at the heart of the club's rise from mediocrity to being an Italian phenomenon and a European power, while also never being far from disappointment and controversy. There were tears as Mancini said farewell, from the player himself, and the fans, and two days later he was gone, signed by Lazio for £3.2 million just as Eriksson joined the Roman club.

Crucially, the Rome club's president Sergio Cragnotti had promised Mancio a place on the coaching staff when he hung up his boots. Mancini moved to an ambitious club in that summer of 1997 – Lazio also made a bold attempt to buy Brazilian ace Ronaldo, then the world's best player, from Barcelona as Cragnotti waved his cheque-book. As Mancini went to work at his new club, there were whispers of a possible treble as, after an average start which had some fans calling for Eriksson's head, Lazio embarked on a 15-match unbeaten run in Serie A, their title interest only ending with a home defeat by eventual winners Juventus in April.

Mancini was handed the valued number ten shirt, seen in Italy as the preserve of the man who makes the team tick. For the first time in his career, he played in every league game, and he got his Lazio career off to a great start with a goal on his Serie A debut for the "Biancocelesti" (sky blue and whites) in a 2–0 home win over Napoli. In competition with Alen Boksic, Pierluigi Casiraghi and Giuseppe Signori for two or three striking places, Mancio was no longer the main striker, and only managed nine goals, his lowest total for ten years. But as the season evolved, Eriksson began to use him as a trequartista or attacking midfielder, in behind the two strikers as a creative force, and it worked beautifully.

Mancio worked his way into the hearts of the Lazio fans with a brilliant goal and an assist for Casiraghi in the ferocious Derby della Capitale, as Roma were beaten 3–1 at the Stadio Olimpico, the ground shared by the two Roman clubs. The league defeat by Juve in April ended their title ambitions, but by that point Lazio were in the Coppa Italia final and 90 minutes away from booking a place in the Uefa Cup final. Days after the defeat at Juve, Lazio went to San Siro for the first leg of the Coppa Italia final against Milan, and lost to a last-minute George Weah goal. When Demetrio Albertini scored in the second leg at the Olimpico, Lazio's dream of lifting only their second Coppa Italia seemed to have been dashed. But Mancini unselfishly set up Guerino Gottardi for the equalizer, Jugovic scored from the penalty spot to bring the aggregate scores level, and defender Alessandro Nesta scrambled in the winner to send 70,000 fans wild. Mancini had his fifth Coppa Italia winners' medal, equalling the record, but he had already turned his gaze towards the Uefa Cup final, in Paris the following week.

Lazio had breezed through to the semi-finals of the European competition, with straightforward wins over Vitoria Guimaraes, Rotor Vologograd, Rapid Vienna and Auxerre, but they faced a lively Atletico Madrid in the last four. Jugovic settled it with the only goal of the two ties, in Madrid, and Lazio were in their first European final, where they would face familiar opposition, in the shape of Inter, at the Parc des Princes in Paris. Boksic was injured, so Mancini partnered Casiraghi up front against an Inter side which had finished as league runners-up and boasted a cosmopolitan all-star team which included Brazil's Ronaldo. It was his Chilean strike partner Ivan Zamorano who broke the deadlock, and when Javier Zanetti and Ronaldo added further goals, it was another European night of misery for Mancio. Lazio were paying the price for chasing trophies on three fronts – they had been physically and mentally exhausted by the time they reached Paris.

But the 1997–98 season had been a promising start to Lazio's bid for domination, buoyed up by their flotation on the Stock Exchange, the first by an Italian club. That handed Cragnotti the funds to build, and in the summer of 1998 they splashed out a breathtaking £89 million, the biggest spending spree in football history, on strikers Christian Vieri and Marcelo Salas, Sinisa Mihajlovic, Dejan Stankovic, Ivan de la Pena, Sergio Conceicao and Fernando Couto.

They got off to a great start in the new season, Mancini setting up Conceicao for a last-minute winner in the Supercoppa curtain-raiser. But three wins from the first 11 games was not title form, and after they had tossed away a 3–1 lead in the Rome derby to draw 3–3, a dressing-room meeting was called. Mancini had scored twice as Salas's strike partner in the Olimpico, but he believed it was time for a change, and was duly moved back to play as trequartista behind Vieri and Salas. The season simply took off as Lazio put together a 16-match unbeaten run. By the beginning of April they were six points clear at the top of the league with seven games to play, and in the semi-finals of the Cup Winners' Cup. The run had seen Mancini at his inspirational best, and at Parma, in a 3–1 win, he scored perhaps his greatest goal. It came from a Mihajlovic corner, delivered with typical ferocity and curve towards the near post. Mancini made the run to the near post, but the cross was too low to head, so he improvised, with a leap and a back-heel which sent the ball flashing past a stunned Parma goalkeeper. It has been voted the best goal ever scored by an Italian.

Lazio wrapped up one trophy before the end of the domestic season by lifting the Cup Winners' Cup, the last time the competition was held, before it was absorbed by the Uefa Cup. Lazio's ordinary early-season form meant they had squeezed through against Lausanne and Partisan Belgrade, but by the quarter-finals they were in imperious shape. Greek outfit Panionios were dismissed 7–0 on aggregate, and then Lokomotiv Moscow were beaten on the away goals rule in the semi-final, with Mancini's delicate back-heel setting up Boksic for the vital away goal in a 1–1 draw in Moscow.

But the European distraction affected Lazio, and by the time they had reached the final, the lead over Milan in the league was down to one point. Both teams won their next three, but with the Cup Winners' Cup final looming, Lazio could only draw at Fiorentina while Milan won to snatch top spot. There was some respite for the shocked Biancocelesti as they beat Real Mallorca in the final, held at Villa Park in Birmingham, with goals from Vieri and Pavel Nedved either side of Dani's equalizer. There was little time to celebrate, as the final day of the Serie A season was just four days away, and Lazio had to beat Parma and hope Milan slipped up at Perugia. Mancini and Co. did their job with a 2–1 victory, but Oliver Bierhoff scored the vital goal as Milan lifted the title. The newspaper headlines were cruel. "Milan win Lazio's title" was one of them, hammering home the fact that Eriksson's men had let a big lead slip.

Now at least the fans believed in the revolution of Eriksson and Cragnotti, even when Vieiri left in the summer of 1999 after a row with the president. Eriksson told his boss that if he brought him

Veron from Parma, he would deliver the title. The proceeds of the world record £31 million sale of Vieiri brought in both Veron and Simone Inzaghi, while Diego Simeone joined too as part of the Vieiri deal. Lazio's rise into the Champions League also coincided with a lucrative new TV deal signed by the seven elite Italian clubs – Juve, Inter, Milan, Lazio, Roma, Parma and Fiorentina.

With a huge squad of big names, and a possible 17 matches in the Champions League, Eriksson had to introduce a rotation policy in an effort to keep everyone happy, and that was another valuable lesson which Mancini soaked up. They began by lifting some silverware, as Mancini had his first encounter with Manchester United in the European Super Cup, held in Monaco. A goal from Salas was enough to see off the Red Devils.

The 1999–2000 season was to be a glorious one for Lazio, but one in which Mancini, who celebrated his 35th birthday, realized he was coming to the end of his powers. For the first time in his career, he failed to score a Serie A goal, but that fact was lost in the euphoria of the title win. However, his precision passing and shooting was not entirely wasted. The day after Lazio lost the Rome derby 4–1 to Fabio Capello's Roma, the Formello training ground was besieged by 200 angry Lazio ultras. When some began to climb the fence and abuse individual players they blamed for the humiliation, Mancini repelled the assault by kicking balls at them.

By February, hopeful Lazio eyes were again being cast towards a treble, as they were top of Serie A, well placed to qualify from their Champions League group, and in the Coppa Italia semi-finals. They had also been reinforced by Lombardo, who joined in January to end an English adventure which had made him the idol of Crystal Palace fans. The assault on three trophies began well as Mancini scored twice in a 5–0 win over Venezia in the first leg of the domestic cup semi-final. But the tiring schedule of league, cup and Europe again began to take its toll, and by the middle of March Lazio were nine points behind leaders Juventus and needed to win at Chelsea to be sure of staying in the Champions League.

They pulled that off, winning 2–1 at Stamford Bridge and, rejuvenated, set off on an eight-match unbeaten run which took them to the Serie A title. The Champions League dream was ended by Valencia in the quarter-finals, but the domestic double was still in sight, and there was big news for Mancini on March 30, 2000. As Lazio prepared for a crunch with Juventus which could chop the Bianconeri's lead to three points, Cragnotti kept the promise he had made to Mancini when he signed, elevating the player to the coaching staff, as Eriksson's assistant. Mancio wasted no time, taking the Lazio players for training on the day before the big game.

Cragnotti thought Mancini would be better suited to the role of sporting director, the man who in a typical Italian club makes the deals, fashions the team and sorts out contracts, rather than a track-suited coach, but predicted he would have "a bright career on the bench". As Lazio beat Zinedine Zidane's Juventus 1–0, Mancini was sitting in the stand, taking notes, rather than delivering pinpoint passes. He still donned his boots in the closing weeks of the season, usually as a substitute, but his Italian career turned full circle when he began the last away game of his career in Italy, at Bologna, where it had all begun almost 19 years earlier. It was a crucial game as well, Lazio needing to win to remain two points behind Juve with a game left. Mancini played his part, with a cross which fell for Conceicao to equalize on the way to a nervy 3–2 victory.

Now the situation was simple. To win the league, Lazio had to beat Reggina and hope Juve would slip up at lowly Perugia. Mancini had worshipped Juve as a boy, and now they stood between him and a glorious end to a glittering career. Bitter experience had soured his idealistic boyhood view of Juventus, who consistently seemed to get favourable treatment by referees. (It was a suspicion which would be vindicated six years later when it became clear that the Turin giants had been manipulating officials.) In their penultimate game, Juve had benefited from a curious refereeing decision which had denied Parma's Fabio Cannavaro an equalizer with the last touch of the game, the referee claiming he had blown the whistle before the defender's header hit the net. If the goal had stood, the two teams would have entered the final day of the season level on points. Lazio fans rioted after hearing of Parma's ghost goal, and protested on the final day by staging a mock funeral for Italian football, complete with a coffin.

An incensed Mancini said in the days before the crunch match, in words dripping with meaning: "I am proud to have played in three teams, Bologna, Sampdoria and Lazio, who have never received favours at crucial moments." He also stirred a hornets' nest by suggesting Sampdoria's Scudetto nine years earlier had been the last "true" triumph in the competition – a hint that Milan and Juventus, who had shared the titles since, had unfair advantages.

Ironically, it was Lazio who got all the lucky breaks in a controversial climax to the season, but it seemed more likely to be due to divine intervention than anything sinister. Lazio took advantage of two soft refereeing decisions for Inzaghi and Veron to both score from the penalty spot and put them 2–0 up at half time, while a nervous Juve were goalless at half time in Perugia. During the break, the heavens opened in Perugia and the start of the second half had to be delayed, with the pitch flooded. There had been an agreement to co-ordinate the timing of the two games to avoid accusations of wrongdoing, so Lazio also had to wait to resume their game, until referee Gennaro Borriello ran out of patience and began again. Simeone scored a third, and then anxious Lazio players and fans waited for news from Perugia. It was good news – hampered by the stress of the situation and the dreadful conditions, Juve slipped to defeat, and Lazio had won the Scudetto, only the second in their history. The victory was credited to Eriksson's rotation policy, which kept his players fresher in the run-in.

Mancini was carried around the pitch by Lombardo, tears in his eyes, but he still had one last achievement in mind before he ended his playing career in Italy. Three days after the Scudetto win, Lazio had the second leg of the Coppa Italia, and led Inter 2–1 from the first leg at the Olimpico. Two tired teams played out a goalless draw, in which Mancini played for the first half, and his last game on Italian soil saw him pick up a record sixth Coppa Italia winners' medal as Lazio celebrated a historic double.

His playing days in Italy were over, and he hung up his boots, with plenty to show for his distinguished career: two Scudetti, two Cup Winners' Cup medals, six Coppa Italias, two Italian Super Cups and one European Super Cup.

The 2000–01 season began and Mancini threw himself into his new role as assistant to Eriksson, while there were already rumours that Fiorentina had one eye on his talent. Mancini was content, for the time being, to be the Swede's sidekick, especially as another spending spree brought in Hernan Crespo, Claudio Lopez, Dino Baggio and goalkeeper Angelo Peruzzi, as the Romans eyed an

assault on the Champions League. But just three games into the new
season, Eriksson announced he would be leaving Lazio at the end
of the season to manage England. Cragnotti considered Mancini
as a possible successor, but he had only just begun to study for his
coaching qualifications, and was not due to take his first badge until
the summer of 2001.

Things came to a head in January 2001, when Lazio were down in
fifth place, 11 points off the lead, had crashed out of the Coppa Italia
to Udinese and had suffered successive defeats in their Champions
League group, to Anderlecht and Leeds United. Cragnotti fired
Eriksson, and when it became clear he would not be offered the job,
Mancini also walked.

That brought about perhaps the most curious episode of
Mancio's glittering career. Within a week of walking out of Lazio,
he had resurrected his playing career in the unlikely surroundings
of Leicester City, in the English Premier League. Leicester were
managed by Peter Taylor, a friend of Eriksson, and were over-
achieving at sixth in the table. Mancini's reasoning for the move was
simple: "I've been playing football with my kids but it's not easy for
someone like me, after 24 years of the pitch and the dressing-room,
to stay and do nothing. I am back to play for six months in England,
and want to hear what Leicester have to say. This is an experience
that will be very useful for my career. I hope to learn from playing
here and working with Peter Taylor because I want the experience to
help me for the future as a coach and manager."

His old Sampdoria partner Gianluca Vialli, who ended his
successful playing career at Chelsea, and had just been sacked as
their coach, had urged Mancio to try English football. Eriksson
had recommended him to Taylor, and on January 18, he signed a

one-month contract with a view to remaining until the end of the season.

Taylor told the Leicester Mercury: "He is a lovely fellow, he's very knowledgeable about a lot of our players already, fitted in well in the training, which was quite light anyway, and then went away with a few videos of our games to get to know even more about how we play. Of course, he knows that, as he is 36 years old, I am looking for his football intelligence, not his legs. There will be enough young legs around him so that should be all right. And he also understands that his role will be to help bring through the younger men and pass on his experience to the other strikers. I am optimistic that this could work out well and he will definitely be in the 16 for Saturday."

Taylor would be among the first to congratulate Mancini on his appointment at Manchester City in 2009, and recalled his brief stay in the east Midlands: "I thought Roberto was a diamond of a man you could trust. He was a magnificent player who was coming to the end of his career when I signed him. But he wanted to have a look at the English scene. I did not have a clue at that stage that he would go on to manage in Italy and win the things he has as a manager. But what I did notice was that he knew about training and he showed an interest in the way we trained at Leicester. I know he is serious about what he does and if he does anything, he does it well."

Mancini made his Leicester debut against Arsenal at Filbert Street, no doubt experiencing a bit of a culture shock. He had gone from sharing a dressing-room with Veron, Nesta and Mihajlovic to mixing with Muzzy Izzet, Gerry Taggart and Robbie Savage, who became his room-mate and remains a friend. The opposition was more illustrious, with Patrick Vieira and future City man Sylvinho in the Gunners' line-up, but Mancini played 76 minutes and helped his side to a 0–0 draw. He then contributed to an FA Cup win at Aston Villa – his only playing appearance in the competition – after which he turned out in a 1–0 defeat at Southampton and helped his new side beat Chelsea, a performance which prompted David Lacey of the Guardian to observe that he "looked like a bottle of Frascati which had found itself in the company of brown ales".

Mancini was starting to look more like his old self when he almost staged a second-half fightback as the Foxes went down 2–1 at Everton. The Italian was thrown on at half time with his side two goals down, and a trademark pass led to Dean Sturridge's late goal, but it was to be the last game of his cameo career in England. The definitive Leicester City history Of Fossils and Foxes puts it thus: "Roberto exuded veteran class for City, but was to find that getting his temporary team-mates onto the same quick-thinking wavelength was no easy task."

So, Mancio's playing days did not end, as befitted his ability, on a sun-kissed day in Lombardy, hoisting another trophy to the heavens and receiving the adulation of his fans. They came to a close on a grim, grey day at Goodison Park, in a mid-table scrap between Everton and Leicester City, in February 2001. This is how Leicester boss Peter Taylor summed up the game which brought Mancini's playing days to a close: "They steamed into us in the first half and we didn't steam into them, and it cost us."

It was a far cry from the artistry of Il Mancio, and the technical and tactical excellence of a classic Serie A encounter, but Mancini had long been an admirer of English football.

Chapter Five
Riots, Rogues and Redemption

Roberto Mancini's management career began amid burning police cars and rioting fans, serving two club owners who would both end up behind bars. Those unpredictable, crazy days at Fiorentina and Lazio, as Italian football careered into a crisis of bankruptcy, fan violence and corruption, were a far cry from the relative tranquillity, financial security and shining silverware of his later days at Inter Milan and then Manchester City. But they helped to forge the man who took the Nerazzurri to a hat-trick of Serie A titles before leading City out of the wilderness and invading neighbours United's "promised land".

Mancini returned to Italy after his final game at Everton, ostensibly to go to the Italian FA's technical centre at Coverciano as part of his ongoing coaching course. Leicester believed he would be rejoining them after a short break, but Mancini was finished with playing. When Fiorentina's highly rated Turkish coach Fatih Terim quit, club president Vittorio Cecchi Gori invited Mancini to take the post. They ran into an immediate problem, as Italian FA rules stated that no-one could be employed by two clubs in the same season, and Mancini was still registered as a coach at Lazio.

The head of the coaches' association was Mancini's old national team coach, Azeglio Vicini, who had felt the sharp edge of his tongue

more than once, and he protested strongly that Mancini should
not be allowed to "trample on the rules" that every other coach
had to adhere to. The other coaches were also unhappy that a man
who had yet to take his coaching badge would be allowed to take
charge of a Serie A team. The Italian FA finally ruled in Fiorentina's
favour, on the basis that Mancini had only been an assistant coach,
and Vicini resigned in disgust. But Mancini was free to take up
his first job as head coach and was appointed by Fiorentina on
March 8, 2001.

The youngest coach in Serie A had walked straight into a
political and financial battlefield. Terim was hugely popular among
the Fiorentina fans as he had the team punching above its weight
and had already booked a place in the Coppa Italia final. He was
being lined up by AC Milan and had sensed the financial crisis
which was about to envelop the Florence club. The Viola's main
assets were being sold, with Argentina striker Gabriel Batistuta
having already gone to Roma in the summer of 2000. President
Cecchi Gori, an award-winning film producer, had "borrowed"
£25 million of club profits to prop up his other ailing businesses,
and by the summer of 2001 had already spent the television
income for the next two seasons, plus the season ticket revenue
until 2006.

Fiorentina were in 11th place without a win in seven games
when Mancini took the reins, but on the plus side they still had
the brilliant Portuguese midfielder Manuel Rui Costa and Italy
goalkeeper Francesco Toldo, while Mancini's old Sampdoria and Italy
strike partner Enrico Chiesa led the line. Mancini had also inherited
an end-of-season showpiece, as the Viola were already through to
face Parma in the final of the Coppa Italia.

Fiorentina drew his first game in charge, at Perugia, and went on a run of just one defeat in his first seven matches, which had them five points away from a Uefa Cup place by the beginning of May. Rui Costa later admitted he had been pleasantly surprised by his new boss: "As a footballer he was always number one, a champion respected by all – team-mates and opponents. I have to admit that I was curious to get to know Mancini the coach. On the pitch he was, you might say, a bit arrogant. He had achieved enough in his career that he felt entitled to a certain degree of attention. Or at least I saw things that way. But when he arrived at Fiorentina I discovered a simple man who dispensed with formalities, who created a positive atmosphere. He spoke with people, he listened, he asked questions. He was neither afraid nor preoccupied, he just had a great desire to get started."

League form tailed away but Mancini still guided his new club into the Uefa Cup by landing the Coppa Italia, a competition with which his name was already synonymous as a player. To make it sweeter, the team they beat in the two-leg final, Parma, was coached by Renzo Ulivieri, Mancini's his first boss at Sampdoria.

In the summer, Mancini threw himself into earning his coaching qualifications at the Italian FA's technical centre at Coverciano, appropriately writing his thesis about the role of the *trequartista*, a role he coveted but had so often been denied. Just down the road in Florence, Cecchi Gori was holding a fire sale as the iconic Rui Costa, darling of the Stadio Franchi fans, was snapped up by Milan for £37 million, and keeper Toldo went to Inter for £23 million. Having cashed in on the best assets, Cecchi Gori put the club up for sale, and failed to provide reinforcements.

The Fiorentina players began the 2001–02 season having not been paid since July and not surprisingly didn't fare well, with five defeats from the opening seven matches, followed by an exit from the Coppa Italia at the hands of Serie B side Como. The gloom was deepened by the loss of Chiesa, whose season was ended when he suffered ruptured knee ligaments in a game against Venezia in September after he had scored five goals in the opening five matches.

By November the unpaid players were in revolt. Captain Angelo di Livio revealed they were ready to sue the club for breach of contract, which would have given Fiorentina 20 days to find the money for their wages or be obliged to release the entire squad on free transfers. As the club threatened to fall apart, Cecchi Gori was otherwise occupied – he was hauled out of bed, along with his young actress girlfriend, in a dawn raid by police investigating allegations of false accounting, embezzlement, fraud and cocaine possession. He was also fighting a £40 million divorce case in the USA.

Mancini was desperate for players and appeared to have pulled off a mini-coup by arranging loan deals to bring in Brazilian striker Adriano from Inter and his old Lazio team-mate Sinisa Mihajlovic, only for the club to pull the plug on both deals. Defeat by Perugia sparked riots by 2,000 Fiorentina ultras, who tried to storm the dressing-room and had to be dispersed by tear gas. Mancini left the stadium with a police escort and the following day offered his resignation. It was turned down, and Mancini was given a promise that money would be found to bring in two or three players.

After meeting Cecchi Gori in Rome to discuss the problems, Mancini returned home to Florence, only to be accosted outside the house by four ultras who he said "verbally assaulted" him – they later claimed that they simply tried to let him know their feelings, and offered no threat. Fearing for his wife and three children, Mancini quit in January 2002. Fiorentina would be relegated and go bankrupt that summer, before being re-invented in Serie C and fighting their way back into Serie A within two seasons.

Mancini's first taste of management had been traumatic, but now he had to find another job. Lazio moved quickly and by the end of April, Mancini was lined up for a £680,000 a year post, with the incentive of a £60,000 bonus for reaching the Champions League. His coaching staff would be familiar to Manchester City fans – he appointed Ivan Carminati, who had worked with Mancini the player under Eriksson, as fitness conditioner, and Massimo Battara as goalkeeping coach. Nando Orsi would be Mancini's assistant.

Lazio were a star-studded outfit boasting internationals like Argentina's Hernan Crespo, Italy stalwart Alessandro Nesta, and ex-Manchester United defender Jaap Stam, but had only sneaked into sixth place, and a Uefa Cup place, by beating Inter on the final day of the season. Mancini, always popular as a Lazio player, was presented to the fans at the Formello training ground on May 10, days after the end of the season, and was greeted with adulation by 5,000 of them. But this was a different Lazio from the club for which he had played – in those golden days the stock market flotation and Cragnotti's limitless ambition had thrust them into the Italian elite. Now there was payback, and there were already dark rumblings about the squad being down-sized and the wage bill trimmed as Cragnotti's tinned food company Cirio – which owned 51 per cent of Lazio – plunged into crisis.

Bold talk of buying Rivaldo from Barcelona or bringing Veron back from his unhappy spell at Manchester United came to nothing, but in the summer of 2002, while Mancini sunned himself on his yacht off the coast of Sardinia, his favourite holiday destination, the Lazio fans were brimming with optimism for the new season.

But the football fates were again conspiring. Clubs around the world had begun to call in money owed from Cragnotti's wild spending. Manchester United were demanding £12 million they were still owed for Stam; Brazilian side Cruzeiro wanted the irst instalment for Juan Pablo Sorin; and Valencia were demanding payments for the £30 million purchase of Gaizka Mendieta, who had already flopped and been sent to Barcelona on loan. Fifa banned Lazio from buying or selling abroad until the matter was settled, and the Italian FA threatened to tear up the contracts for two domestic signings, Massimo Oddo and Christian Manfredini, unless payments were made.

On the first transfer deadline day in football history, August 31, 2002, the bomb dropped. Crespo and Nesta, the two biggest names at Lazio, were both sold, the Argentine striker going to Inter in a £32 million deal which saw Bernardo Corradi go the other way, and Nesta – who had been at the club since he was nine – going to AC Milan for £27 million. It was too much for the fans, and after a friendly against Juventus the following day, they rioted, burning three police cars, ransacking club offices and stabbing three visiting supporters.

Mancini told his players to focus on their game, and despite the fact they had not been paid since June, Lazio went on a 16-match unbeaten run in the league. By Christmas they were second, a point behind joint leaders AC Milan and Inter, in the last 16 of the Uefa Cup and in the quarter-finals of the Coppa Italia. Claudio Lopez, who had failed to score a league goal in an injury-hit first season at the Olimpico, hit 15 goals from 30 starts. Mancini also resurrected the career of other players who seemed to have hit a wall in Italy – Corradi would flop at Manchester City four years later, but provided valuable back-up to Lopez with 11 goals, while 33-year-old Mihajlovic was a revelation.

The financial crisis overflowed in November after Cirio, the food company which owned Lazio, defaulted on more than £660 million of bonds. Lazio had made it seven away wins from seven by beating Juventus on December 15, but the frustration of the players boiled over as they demanded the backlog of unpaid wages be paid. The club's main creditor, the Capitalia bank, insisted that Cragnotti stand down with the club £130 million in debt, and Sorin was sold to Barcelona in the winter transfer window. Mancini's guidance had the team pressing on three fronts, but fans did not know whether to be exhilarated by what was happening on the pitch, or anxious about what was happening off it.

The bank consortium drafted Mancini onto an emergency three-man board to run the troubled club, making him into an English-style general manager in the process. Such a role, combining coaching duties with wider responsibility for transfers, contracts and the development of the entire playing side, was unique at the top level in Italy where the roles of coach and sporting director are sharply defined.

With the financial crisis seemingly easing, Lazio hit a rocky patch. The unbeaten run finally came to an end in a 1–0 defeat at Reggina, and they promptly went nine matches without a league win to slide out of the title race.

Mancini was already being targeted by Inter at this point, the Milan giants impressed by the way he had kept Lazio on track amid the chaos of the club's financial turmoil, but he was focusing on an intense spell of seven games in three weeks which could still bring some respite to the beleaguered club. The dream of winning the Uefa Cup was ended by another thrusting young manager, José Mourinho. His impressive Porto side destroyed Lazio 4–1 in Portugal in the first leg of the semi-final, despite Lopez giving the Italians the lead, and then held them 0–0 at the Olimpico. In between those games, Lazio also exited the Coppa Italia at the hands of Roma.

Free from cup distractions, Mancini's side staged a strong finish to the season which guaranteed a Champions League place, and with it a huge boost for empty club coffers. The confidence in Lazio shares brought about by the new board's restructuring plan, and the success on the field, was also helping to heal financial wounds. At the end of a traumatic, terrific season, Lazio and the Capitalia bank persuaded Mancini to sign a new five-year contract, promising him money for new signings and that stars like Stam and Dejan Stankovic would not be sold.

Mancini gave Lazio another boost ahead of the league season by guiding his side past a tricky Champions League qualifier against Benfica to reach the lucrative group stages, but Lazio soon became a model of inconsistency – and seemed to reserve their worst performances for big European nights. A 2–1 defeat by Chelsea at Stamford Bridge, inspired by Mancini's old Lazio team-mate Veron, put them on the back foot. And when Chelsea went to the Olimpico and shocked the faithful with a 4–0 win, they were on their way out. To make matters worse Mihajlovic, never far from controversy, was sent off for chopping down Damien Duff, and then compounded his disgrace by spitting at Adrian Mutu and throwing a plastic bottle towards a Uefa official who tried to usher him away from the tunnel area. Mancini, perhaps remembering his own transgressions as a player, tried to play down the incident, and then deliberately deflected criticism for the heavy defeat onto his own shoulders, a ploy he likes to use at Manchester City to ease pressure on his players.

Mancini confidently predicted Lazio would win their final two group games to qualify, but they were held at home by Besiktas and lost to Sparta in Prague to end their campaign. Dissent rumbled around the Olimpico amid fresh financial troubles and talk of a player sell-off. Stankovic had already declared he was leaving for Inter, so Lazio prepared to sell him in the transfer window rather than lose him for nothing when his contract expired the following summer. Faced with more financial juggling and the loss of key players, Mancini said he regretted his decision to stay and made it plain he would be quitting in June, leading to talks with Tottenham Hotspur at one point.

In his frustration Mancini said, with apparent prescience which still only hinted at the luxury of life at Inter and Manchester City: "First of all I was at Fiorentina and we couldn't buy anyone. Now I'm at Lazio and we can't buy anyone. Some day I'd like to be in a position where I can buy some players, then we could win something."

The extent of the financial scandal which had enveloped the club was revealed on February 11, when Cragnotti was arrested for his part in the crash of the Cirio food company. He would end up being sentenced to nine years in prison.

As they prepared for the first leg of the Coppa Italia semi-final against Juventus, Lazio announced losses of £46 million and club shares were suspended on the Milan stock exchange. Once more Mancini led his troops to victory in the face of off-field disaster, beating Juve with two Stefano Fiore goals. The coach was intent on leaving Lazio fans with a parting gift of a Coppa Italia triumph. He duly delivered, securing his second as a manager, by leading his team to a 2–2 draw at Juventus for a 4–2 aggregate at the end of the season. Lazio flew back into Rome at 3.30 in the morning to be greeted at the airport by over 3,000 fans, all chanting in vain for Mancini to stay.

By that point, Mancio's only fear was that he might get trampled in the rush for the exit door. A saviour was around the corner for Lazio in the shape of businessman Claudio Lotito, who prevented a Fiorentina-style bankruptcy, but it was too late to keep Mancini and his star players as captain Giuseppe Favalli and Mihajlovic joined him at Inter, and Lopez, Stam, Fiore and Corradi also abandoned ship.

Mancini was announced as the new Inter coach on July 7, 2004 on a three-year contract – after years of trying to sign Mancio as a player, Inter owner Massimo Moratti had finally got his man as coach. He was walking out of a crisis club and into one whose fans simply thought they were in a crisis. Since Giovanni Trapattoni had led Inter to the Serie A title in 1989, the domestic league had become a wasteland for Inter, even though they had won three Uefa Cups in the 15 intervening years. What made matters worse was that rivals AC Milan, with whom they share the San Siro stadium, had won six league titles, three Champions Leagues and a Coppa Italia in that same period. The comparisons between football in the cities of Milan and Manchester are irresistible – Inter had not experienced anything as desolate at City's 35 years without any trophy or 44 years without winning the league, but their fans, like Manchester's Blues, still hankered after the glory days of the Sixties and early Seventies when they won two European Cups and three league titles and were not constantly having their noses rubbed in the dirt by ultra-successful neighbours. When Mancini moved in at Inter, their city rivals were crowing about their latest title triumph, when they had racked up a record points total. Mancini's mission, which had already proved beyond a series of top managers – including Roy Hodgson, Marcello Lippi and Hector Cuper – was to knock Milan off their perch.

Mancini was not daunted – he was finally at a club where he had money to spend, top-quality players, and no pressure to sell. First, as usual, he tightened things up at the back, bringing in ex-Lazio boys Mihajlovic and Favalli, as well as Argentina international defender Nicolas Burdisso, and gave his midfield backbone by picking up Edgar Davids from Barcelona and Esteban Cambiasso from Real Madrid. There was little wrong with his attacking options of Christian Vieri, Obafemi Martins and Alvaro Recoba, and his decision to bring back Adriano from Parma was to prove a masterstroke. Three more new boys, Stankovic, Ze Maria and on-loan Veron, added guile to midfield, but Mancini knew he still didn't have a team to challenge for the title.

He made his team hard to beat – they set a new Italian record by going 38 matches unbeaten in all competitions from the start of the season. That was enough to see them to the brink of the Champions League quarter-finals and into the Coppa Italia semi-finals. But they were drawing too many games to sustain a title challenge – 16 of their first 25 league games ended in stalemate so they were trailing leaders Milan by 11 points when Kaka's goal ended their incredible unbeaten run in the Milan derby on February 27. The Champions League was proving much smoother for Mancini and his team, as they eased to qualification, the highlight being a 5–1 thrashing of Valencia on their own ground, but a last 16 win over Porto booked a Champions League quarter-final … against Milan.

Before that, Mancini had to run the gauntlet of going back to Lazio, having recently sued his former club for non-payment of £610,000 in salary and bonuses. The Roman club's new owner Claudio Lotito retorted by reporting his former coach to the Italian FA, and claiming £3.5 million damages, for alleged "disloyal behaviour". Mancini drew the match and won his court case, while Lotito's claims were dismissed.

Adriano was injured for the Champions League clash with Milan, and Inter slumped to a 2–0 defeat in the first leg. Two losses in 39 games might satisfy some supporters, but when they are both inflicted by your deadliest rivals, who are 14 points clear of you in the league, it hurts. And when Andriy Shevchenko's goal in the second leg made defeat virtually certain, the reaction of the Inter fans in the 79,000 crowd was appalling. They bombarded Milan keeper Dida with flares, one hitting him on the shoulder, and the game was abandoned. It was awarded 3–0 to Milan by the governing body Uefa. Inter escaped a ban but picked up a record £132,000 fine and were ordered to play their next four European games behind closed doors.

Recalling the fortitude in adversity shown in his days at Fiorentina and Lazio, Mancini rallied his players to win seven of their last eight league games to finish third, clinching Champions League football. He also reinforced his reputation as "Mr Coppa Italia" by taking his team to triumph in the final, their first for 23 years, and his ninth as player and coach. Adriano scored both goals in a 2–0 win in the first leg at Roma, and Mihajlovic lashed in a trademark 30-yard free kick in the second leg to land Mancio his first trophy as Inter coach.

Inter reinforced in the summer of 2005 by making Veron's loan permanent and by bringing in three Real Madrid stars – tough Argentina central defender Walter Samuel, 32-year-old Luis Figo, and midfielder Santiago Solari. Playmaker David Pizarro, later to join up with Mancini at City, also moved to Inter from Udinese. The season began on a positive note as Inter eased into the Champions League group stage with a qualifying victory over Shakhtar Donetsk, the home leg played in an empty San Siro as Uefa's punishment began, and Veron's extra-time goal brought victory over reigning champions Juventus in the season-opening Supercoppa. It was to be a season remembered for all the wrong reasons, and ended with Inter taking their first Scudetto for 17 years in unsatisfying circumstances as the Calciopoli match-fixing scandal broke like a storm on Italian football.

With Veron and Figo finding vintage form, Cambiasso supporting their clever passing game and Samuel shoring up the defence, Inter began the season strongly and sports newspaper *Gazzetta* declared that Mancini's team were potentially "the greatest Inter ever". But there were problems stacking up with the party-loving Adriano. He took four days to get back from international duty with Brazil, arriving at the San Siro ten minutes before the end of a 5–0 win over Livorno. Depressed by the death of his father and a split from his pregnant girlfriend, Adriano then skipped a training session and put in his worst performance of the season in a 2–2 draw with Sampdoria. Mancini watched that match from the stands after receiving a two-match touchline ban for abusing a referee. Team discipline appeared to be in tatters in a goalless draw with Lazio, as Alvaro Recoba angrily walked away from the bench and went home when he was left as an unused substitute. But again Mancini defied the snipers, his side winning 11 of their next 12 league games and securing a place in the Champions League knockout phase. Adriano found redemption by heading the winner in the Milan derby as Inter tried desperately to close the gap on runaway leaders Juve.

The title race came to a head at San Siro on February 12 in the Derby d'Italia, or Italian derby, as Inter v Juve is known. The hatred of Juventus among Inter fans is far stronger than anything they feel for Milan, and Juve were skipping away with the title, helped by some strange refereeing decisions. Gianluca Paparesta, the referee in a game billed as a title decider, in fact had a good game. He disallowed Adriano's "goal" direct from a free kick after clearly signalling it was indirect, and correctly awarded a free kick for a foul on Pavel Nedved from which Alessandro del Piero struck the winner in a 2–1 Juve victory. Nevertheless Mancini was furious and afterwards made his point about Nedved: "He dives! He always dives that way and you all fall for it!" That outburst, and a verbal attack on Juve official Roberto Bettega, once his boyhood hero, earned him a fine and one-match touchline ban, but the ill-feeling was not at an end.

The next day Figo claimed that Juve sporting director Luciano Moggi had visited the referee's dressing-room before the game, and questioned his presence. Moggi reacted by reporting the Portuguese star to the Italian FA and threatening legal proceedings. Inter backed their player, and relations between the two bitter rivals hit a low. Figo ended up with a £3,300 fine – which he asked to be refunded when Moggi was later arrested as part of the match-fixing scandal.

Ten days later Mancini came to blows with one of his
international stars over a warm-up in a Champions League game,
an uncanny precursor of his row with Carlos Tevez at Manchester
City. The man in question was Marco Materazzi, best known as the
player head-butted by Zinedine Zidane in the 2006 World Cup final.
The 6ft 4in defender had been told to prepare to go onto the field
as Inter drew 2–2 with Ajax in Amsterdam. He did as he was asked,
but when it became clear Mancini was not intending to use him, he
stormed down the tunnel. The two men had a row in the dressing-
room, and had to be separated by other players as they squared up.

Mancini certainly had plenty on his plate at that time – there
were whispers that Inter were seeking to replace him at the end of
the season. Their form was now indifferent and they only won half of
their last dozen matches, losing the Milan derby along the way, to see
their title challenge fizzle out. They also went out of the Champions
League to Villarreal at the quarter-final stage on the away goals rule,
and when Inter arrived back at Malpensa airport from Spain they
were set upon by angry supporters, with Javier Zanetti and Cristiano
Zanetti having to be rescued by police.

The incident made a big impression on Mancini, who had seen
enough of the fan violence which was scarring Italian football. "This
has hastened my plans to go abroad," he was quoted as saying.
"When I am finished with Inter I will leave Italy, that's for sure.
The enjoyment of playing, which is what the game is all about, is
no longer possible. You can't win or lose and think only about what
happens on the field, unfortunately if you lose you have to think
about other things as well."

Inter meandered their way to third place and into another
Coppa Italia final, where they drew at Roma in the first leg before

goals from Cambiasso, Cruz and Martins handed Mancio his tenth Coppa Italia. It was a triumph, but the match was already being overshadowed by events elsewhere, with the biggest scandal in Italian football history about to break.

Italian football supporters, especially those of the smaller clubs, have traditionally been suspicious of the power and influence of the big clubs, especially of Juventus who regularly seemed to get more than their fair share of controversial decisions. Mancini had complained about it during his playing days, but in the summer of 2006 it was revealed that a police investigation had turned the conspiracy theories into a shocking reality. Phone-tapping of Juve owner Luciano Moggi, and other powerful names in the Italian game, revealed a litany of referee coercion, illegal betting, fraud and false accounting.

Mancini, already disillusioned by the burgeoning violence, expressed his desire to escape the whole sorry mess as the storm clouds broke: "If this is true, I won't stay here. I won't stay in Italy with a league where everything is decided. A lot needs to be done to fix this situation, with rules and honest people. Otherwise we should suspend the league, so we don't throw away the money of honest presidents, and go and play in the street instead. People have always talked about this, in bars, for years, but there has been no evidence before. Without all this, I think Inter would have won a few championships."

Juventus went through the pretence of winning the title on May 14, although Moggi resigned and their open-top bus parade through Turin was cancelled. When runners-up Milan were dragged into the scandal, it became likely that Inter would become champions by default. Mancini urged the Italian FA to award the title to Inter, saying it was only right: "If someone wins through cheating in sport, you should reward those who behaved properly. I don't say that because it touches us, but in general."

The Italian national team defied the shame of the scandal to win the 2006 World Cup, but the following week the court delivered the first of its damning verdicts – Juventus would be stripped of the 2004–05 and 2005–06 titles and relegated to Serie B with a 30-point deduction; Lazio and Fiorentina were also relegated with points deductions; and Milan would begin the following season with a 15-point deduction. The punishments to Lazio, Milan and Fiorentina were all later reduced on appeal.

The Italian FA awarded the 2005–06 Scudetto to Inter, a move seen as minimal compensation for the titles which they may have been denied by cheating. As well as picking up an unexpected Scudetto, Inter were also in a position to take advantage of Juve's self-inflicted misfortune – some of their biggest stars were queuing up to leave, and Inter quickly paid £21.8 million for Ibrahimovic and £8.3 million for Vieira. They also snapped up World Cup winner Fabio Grosso, Brazil right back Maicon, and Crespo. With all the big names joining in that tumultuous summer of 2006, the signing of a 16-year-old from Serie C side Lumezzane for £235,000 slipped under the radar. His name was Mario Balotelli.

The vindication of their belief that they had been cheated by Juve and Milan had a profound effect on the psyche of Inter, and possibly of Mancini as well. They suddenly had proof that they had been victims of crime all along – they were not cursed, or inadequate, or paranoid. The banners and chants of the Juve and Milan supporters, mocking Inter's lack of success, disappeared overnight, and with the demons exorcised, they set out with conviction to prove they were the best – it felt like a fresh start. It also helped that Juve were festering in the second division, and Milan, Fiorentina and Lazio all began the season with big points deductions.

Inter began the season as hot favourites, underlined by their thrilling win in the Supercoppa where they hit back from three goals down against Roma, with new boys Vieira (2) and Crespo levelling and Figo grabbing an extra-time winner. But a Champions League defeat at the hands of Sporting Lisbon and indifferent league form brought suggestions that Inter owner Massimo Moratti's notoriously twitchy trigger finger was flexing, and that Mancini had three games to save his job. Inter promptly won at Roma and at home to Chievo to hit top spot before being turned over 2–0 at home by Bayern Munich as Grosso and Ibrahimovic were both red-carded.

Adriano, overweight, unhappy and seeking solace in the bottle, was sent home to Brazil for "physical and psychological" work after skipping another training session, but Crespo and Ibrahimovic, with useful back-up from Cruz and Recoba, made light of the loss as they began to terrorize defences. Inter snapped out of their early-season form and embarked on a stunning run of 17 straight wins, to eclipse Roma's record run of 11 consecutive victories set in the previous season. They were 14 points clear of main rivals Roma when the run ended in February. Adriano had returned to action and had a purple spell of five goals in six games to keep the winning run going, and by the end of January one top Italian bookmaker had already paid out on Inter. The critics were praising Mancini for his transformation from impulsive, instinctive player to methodical, thorough coach. "He is a painter who became a mechanic," wrote one journalist.

After starting the Champions League campaign with two defeats, Inter bounced back in that competition too, beating Spartak Moscow twice, defeating Sporting in the return and then drawing with Bayern in Munich.

Even as he closed in on a second successive title, Mancini was already planning for a future away from Italy. He was learning English and it was not long before he was being linked with Chelsea, as José Mourinho's relationship with owner Roman Abramovich turned sour. But he still had to drive his Inter team home, and there were still troublesome players to handle. Days before the first leg of a last-16 Champions League game with Valencia, Adriano spent two consecutive nights partying with friends, breaking club rules and earning himself a fine, a reprimand and a place on the bench. With Vieira out with a thigh strain, Inter malfunctioned and could only draw 2–2, and when they were held to a goalless draw at the Mestalla, were out of Europe.

The amazing 17-match winning run in the league also came to an end in a 1–1 draw with Udinese, but Inter were still being hailed by fans, media and critics alike as a reincarnation of the great Herrera team of the Sixties. That comparison would bring its own problem, as Herrera had led his team to two European Cups, and Moratti and the Inter fans were already contemplating success in the Champions League. Mancini focused on guiding his team to the title despite the antics of Adriano, whose champagne lifestyle was out of control. After laying on two goals for Ibrahimovic in a 2–1 win at Ascoli, the Brazilian got into a nightclub fight with the giant American basketball player Rolando Howell and landed in more trouble.

Inter could have sealed the Scudetto in fine style with six games still to go had they beaten second-placed Roma at home. But since their European exit Inter had dropped a gear, and they suffered a 3–1 defeat, their first in the league all season, on April 18. That simply delayed the golden moment for a week, however, as Materazzi scored twice in a 2–1 win at Siena and Roma lost at Atalanta. Inter had won the title with five games to go, a Serie A record, and Mancini hailed his players for their "fantastic achievement".

Fans and players joined together in a chorus of "Vinciamo senza rubare!" – meaning "We win without cheating!" The previous season's title had been won by default, but this was a genuine victory, even if it was done without Juve, who were on their way back to the top flight with promotion at the first attempt. Milan's eight-point deduction proved meaningless as they finished 36 points behind – but they still managed to steal some of Inter's thunder by winning the Champions League.

Inter finished the season with four wins from five to head the table by a staggering 22 points, setting three Serie A records along the way – highest points total (97), longest winning streak (17) and most wins in a season (30). However, they blew the chance of another double by folding against Roma in the Coppa Italia final, losing the first leg 6–2 as they ran into Francesco Totti in inspired mood, and winning the second 2–1.

Two titles on the trot could not silence Inter's critics. Juventus fans dismissed the first as victory by default, and were quick to try to devalue the second, as Juve had been absent in the second division. To shut them all up, Inter would have to make it a hat-trick. Mancini did not sit on his hands in the summer of 2007. As well as signing a new deal intended to keep him at the club until 2012, he reinforced his defence with Cristian Chivu and Nelson Rivas, and brought in striker David Suazo.

After losing the Supercoppa to Roma at the start of the 2007–08 season, Inter set off on another breathtaking run, going 25 league games without defeat on their way to a third consecutive title and a fourth Coppa Italia final on the trot. Once again, the fly in the ointment was the Champions League, and an ignominious exit at the hands of Liverpool was to be the beginning of the end for Mancini's reign at Inter. With Ibrahimovic, Cruz, Suazo and Crespo on the books, Adriano had been pushed to one side, and in December he was loaned to Sao Paulo for the rest of the season, with Mancini already keeping a careful eye on 17-year-old Balotelli, who was making waves in the youth team.

Inter's form was patchy in the opening weeks of the season, but with Vieira and Materazzi returning from injuries, and Maicon from a ban, they were 11 points clear of second-placed Roma, in the Coppa Italia semi-finals and the last 16 of the Champions League. The English media feared for Liverpool who had to face Mancini's fearsome side in the Champions League, especially as Moratti had made it plain that his covetous gaze was now focused on prising that trophy from Milan's grasp. The Inter owner had offered the players £260,000 a head for conquering Europe, and Liverpool were the weakest of the four English teams still in the competition.

However, Materazzi was sent off after half an hour, the other central defender Ivan Cordoba suffered a serious knee injury with 15 minutes left, and Liverpool took advantage with late goals from Steven Gerrard and Dirk Kuyt. Mancini was widely criticized in Italy for removing striker Cruz and replacing him with Vieira, who was rusty after several injury problems, and that disappointing night at Anfield appeared to infect Inter's mentality, and cause something to snap inside Mancini.

Interviewed live on television after the game, the wounded Mancini dropped a bombshell, announcing that he thought he would leave at the end of the season. Within 24 hours, Mancio had calmed down and retracted his statement. But his words had stuck in Moratti's mind and he set about replacing his young manager with Mourinho, and publicly expressed his hope that the unguarded words had not compromised Inter's season.

Before the return leg against Liverpool, Inter suffered their first league defeat of the season, at Napoli, and only won one of four league games, as Moratti's fears appeared to be justified. When Fernando Torres's goal handed Liverpool victory in the San Siro second leg – after another harsh red card, this time for Nicolas Burdisso – the air of invincibility which had cloaked Inter for 18 months had suddenly gone. The rest of the season would be a grim struggle to hold off Roma, who now sensed blood. There was more talk of discontent in the dressing-room too, as Ibrahimovic criticized Materazzi for his second yellow card at Anfield, Vieira snubbed Mancini's handshake after being substituted against Sampdoria, and Mancini expressed his displeasure with his own medical staff.

The defeat by Liverpool brought many things to a head, not least Mancini's simmering relationship with Figo. The Portuguese star was on the bench for the game, and – in an uncanny precursor of the infamous Tevez row – refused to listen to Mancini's call, claiming he had already warmed up enough. He stormed out of the stadium after the game.

With his job under threat, the lead in the title race being whittled away, and Ibrahimovic out injured, Mancini turned to an unlikely saviour – a 17-year-old prodigy named Mario Barwuah Balotelli. Given up by his immigrant Ghanaian parents and adopted by an Italian family, the teenager was fast becoming a football prodigy.

The youngster had guided Inter's youth team to their national championship the season before, and had already made his Serie A debut, an uneventful 45 minutes as a substitute at Cagliari in October.

Four goals in two Coppa Italia games, two of them against Juventus, had everyone taking notice. Mancini had predicted he could be a great player, but few expected that, with the title on the line, the coach would pick the rookie striker for a must-win game at Atalanta in April. The teenager responded by planting a corner on Vieira's head for the first goal, and calmly rounding the keeper for the second in a 2–0 win. The following week, Super Mario, as he had now been dubbed by the Italian media, had a hand in Cambiasso's first and again showed remarkable composure to grab the second as Fiorentina were beaten 2–0.

That sparked a run of five league wins and victory over Lazio in the Coppa Italia semi-finals. Balotelli had been a breath of fresh air for his team and the fans were ready to hail a new hero. With three games to go, Inter needed three points to make it a hat-trick of titles. Milan, fighting for a Champions League spot, stood in the way, and goals from Filippo Inzaghi and Kaka instilled some doubt in a 2–1 defeat. Inter would finish the season with a home game against lowly Siena and a trip to relegation-haunted Parma, still needing three points to be sure.

Ahead of the Siena game, Mancini said he was glad the title race had come down to a tight finish: "That way, you appreciate winning it all the more," he said with a smile. But the smile disappeared as Siena grabbed a 2–2 draw, with Materazzi missing a penalty after snatching the ball from designated penalty taker Cruz.

To make matters more intriguing, and more of a parallel to
Manchester City v Mark Hughes's QPR in 2012, last-day opponents
Parma needed to win to avoid relegation and were led by Hector
Cuper, Mancini's predecessor as coach at Inter. Ibrahimovic was due
to return after seven weeks out, and it was a case of cometh the hour,
cometh the man. With the game in the balance, and Roma beating
Catania to seize the initiative, Ibrahimovic was sent on for the second
half, alongside Balotelli, and produced two world-class finishes to
clinch the Scudetto.

The following week Roma gained a modicum of revenge for
defeat in the title race by beating Inter in the Coppa Italia final,
now a one-off game, and it was already clear that Mancini would
get the sack. After winning a hat-trick of titles, and a total of seven
trophies in four seasons at the San Siro, he was heading out of
the door.

The news still shocked Italian football, and the coaches'
association head Renzo Ulivieri, who had been Mancini's first boss at
Sampdoria, leapt to his defence, saying: "The firing of Mancini takes
us all a bit by surprise, considering the results he obtained. As for the
reasons, I'm not well versed on what went on, but listening to them
they seem improbable and even a little presumptuous. The results
speak for Mancini. But this has always been the logic of soccer.
When the environment gets a little overheated, the weakest link pays,
which is the coach."

Ibrahimovic put a new slant on things when he suggested Mancini
had lost the confidence of the dressing-room. "I heard Mancini
and the other coaches talking," he said. "They were worried. The
nervousness had spread through the squad and confidence had
disappeared. From having been a winning machine, we now didn't

even feel confident against the bottom teams. The atmosphere in the team was awful. It was like a switch had been flicked. The harmony and optimism had gone."

Five days after Mancini got the push at Inter, his old mentor Eriksson was fired by Manchester City, to be replaced by Mark Hughes. Within 16 months, Mancini would be the man to succeed Hughes.

Chapter Six
Tearing Down the Red Flag

"When we get to Old Trafford we will take the banner down! It is the last year it will be up, for sure!"

Roberto Mancini's words were bold, or perhaps foolhardy, at the time – but they were to prove beautifully prophetic for the long-suffering Manchester City fans. His team would, 16 months later, force United fans to take down the mocking banner which hung on the Stretford End, intended as a constant reminder of the hopelessness of being a Blue. The banner was designed like a car's milometer, and when Mancini took his post it read, "33 Years" – recording the length of time since City had last won anything of note. The United fans who hung it in a prime spot used to change the number every season that their neighbours went trophy-less. City fans dismissed it as typically arrogant Red nonsense, but secretly many of them loathed it.

When Mancini belied the quiet dignity of his first fortnight as the new City manager with his belligerent words, Blues fans didn't know how to react. Some were thrilled to hear their manager talk in such confident tones of taking on United and rubbing their noses in it, for once. Some cringed inwardly, wishing he would do his talking on the pitch. And many simply shrugged it off as yet another promise by a fly-by-night City manager, which would be lost and forgotten as Typical City found a way to make a mockery of the power afforded them by their newfound wealth and status.

Mancini had walked into Manchester City four days before Christmas in 2009, his first managerial job since being sacked at Inter in May of the previous year, to bring to an end possibly the longest 19 months of his life. In that summer of 2008, in the immediate aftermath of winning a third consecutive title and then being shown the door by Inter, Mancini had found himself in a curious position. He was still on the payroll at the San Siro – unlike English managers, who are simply paid off when they get the push, Italian coaches remain on the payroll until they get a new job, agree a compensation package, or their contract expires. He could have continued to collect his £100,000-plus a week until the summer of 2012 – but that would never have done for someone with his competitive mentality.

He was hurt by his rejection at Inter, perhaps the first major rejection of his football life, and by the reasons given for his sacking, and was not about to go quietly into the Milanese sunset. He issued a statement through his lawyer Stefano Gagliardi that the club's press statement on his sacking had "gravely offended my honour and my reputation", and had referred to "false and illicit events". The lawyer went on to add: "We have a contract which has very clear terms that outline the end of his job, and then there will be a case because this press release has damaged his image both here and abroad."

Until a compensation package was agreed, Mancini was going nowhere, so he set about using his leisure time usefully, as well as taking time out to travel, play tennis, and sail his luxury yacht. He was finding it hard living in Milan, continually being compared to his successor Mourinho – the city simply was not big enough for both of them. It was also the right time for Mancini to leave Italy. He had been sickened by the match-fixing scandal, the fan violence and the financial crimes at Fiorentina and Lazio; and he frequently trumpeted the English game, which he saw as being more entertaining as well as more honest. World stars were no longer heading for Italy, they were all pouring into the Premier League.

There was one moment of bitter-sweet satisfaction for the unemployed Mancini when his fellow coaches voted him the Italian Coach of the Season for guiding Inter to their third successive title. He picked up 60 per cent of the votes and received his award, the Golden Bench, from coaches' association head Azeglio Vicini, ironically the man who had fought so hard to block his first appointment at Fiorentina seven years earlier. He got a warm handshake from his successor at Inter, Mourinho, and told reporters: "I am waiting for something, but at the moment there is nothing on the horizon."

But there was something on the horizon for Mancini, a new business venture. In November 2008 he bought 25 per cent of a new boat-building company, Kifaru, which was 50 per cent owned by the Sarti family, renowned boatyard owners who were already friends of his. He has a passion for yachts dating back to his time in Genoa, and is a regular visitor to boat shows throughout Europe.

He was not contemplating a life away from football. Indeed, during the autumn and winter of 2008 to 2009, he spent a lot of time in London, learning English, steeping himself in the country's football environment and touring training grounds to pick up tips about life in an alien sporting culture. Every English job that became vacant had Mancini's name linked to it, including those at West Ham, Queen's Park Rangers, Fulham and Portsmouth, but he was not interested in taking any backward steps. He wanted a club which could fight for titles, and was prepared to wait. His agent Giorgio de Giorgis told Italian radio: "Until his contract situation is resolved with Inter, Roberto Mancini won't talk to other clubs. That's the way he is."

In February 2009, Luiz Felipe Scolari was fired by Chelsea, and Mancini was immediately cited among the favourites for the job. But his agent insisted there had been no contact from Stamford Bridge, and the London club took on Guus Hiddink as a temporary measure before hiring Carlo Ancelotti in the summer. There was even brief talk of a return to Inter, as Mourinho's position was being questioned after the Nerazzurri crashed out of the Champions League at the last 16 stage, beaten by Manchester United.

That move would have been simple to effect – owner Massimo Moratti would merely have had to recall Mancini, and hold him to his ongoing contract. But both parties quickly poured cold water on the notion. Mancini reiterated that after 30 years of Italian football, he wanted a fresh challenge, preferably in England or Spain.

Sven-Goran Eriksson, his one-time boss at Lazio, wanted Mancini to team up with him once more in the summer of 2009. The former England manager was made director of football at ambitious League Two side Notts County, and wanted his old sidekick as manager. But Mancini's sights were set higher – he was biding his time, waiting for the right job to come along.

Eriksson had initially harboured doubts about Mancini as a manager, suspecting that, like many genius footballers, he might find it hard to cope with coaching and man-managing lesser mortals. But any reservations soon dissolved, and the Swede said: "I was sure that he would impose himself as a manager just like he did as a player. He understands football like few people do. His enthusiasm is contagious and today to overcome the great stress of a league season it's important to have fun training like he does on the pitch."

Doing nothing was never going to be a long-term prospect for someone as driven as Mancini, even if he was guaranteed easy money until his Inter contract expired in the summer of 2012. At the end of October 2009, he reached agreement with his former club, receiving a year's salary of around £5 million, and was again on the market. With Manuel Pellegrini's job under threat after just four months at Real Madrid, Mancini's name was in the frame for that job, but there was another club which had been studying his work at Inter ... nouveau riche Manchester City.

In the summer of 2008, when Mancini was being handed his cards by ungrateful Inter, English football was coming to terms with the shock news that the oil billionaire Sheikh Mansour bin Zayed al Nahyan of Abu Dhabi had taken control of Manchester City. Overnight, the Blues were transformed from long-suffering neighbours of the ultra-successful Manchester United, and perennial mid-table grinders, to the world's richest club. Within 24 hours of taking over, the new owners had made a bold statement of intent, breaking the British transfer record by signing Brazilian superstar Robinho from Real Madrid.

On transfer deadline day manager Mark Hughes returned

from a round of golf to discover he had an expensive new player, and he – and City fans – realized that things would never be the same again. After that signal of intent, the new owner paid out £2.7 million for much-needed improvements to the training and office facilities, and in the next transfer window brought in goalkeeper Shay Given, left back Wayne Bridge, midfielder Nigel de Jong and striker Craig Bellamy for a combined total of £50 million. City finished tenth at the end of their first season under new ownership, and in the summer of 2009 went on a far more serious spree, racking up a bill of £137.5 million to land Carlos Tevez, Emmanuel Adebayor, Joleon Lescott, Roque Santa Cruz, Kolo Touré and Gareth Barry. The owner's business plan, aimed at taking City to the top of English and then European football, included a pledge to eventually have two world-class players for every position in the team.

There was already talk that Hughes was on borrowed time. He had been appointed by the Sheikh's predecessor, the disgraced Thai politician Thaksin Shinawatra, and the new owner, represented by his business lieutenant Khaldoon al Mubarak, had reservations about the Welshman's suitability. Hughes had a good reputation as a man who had lifted Blackburn Rovers away from the threat of relegation and into a Uefa Cup position on a budget. City's new owners needed him to prove that he could handle a top club, which had its sights on league titles and Champions League campaigns, and handle superstar egos rather than English journeymen. The supporters were also not sure about Hughes – his background as a Manchester United star counted against him, and the more impatient fans wanted to see their new-found wealth transformed into success quickly.

Khaldoon, who had taken the post of chairman, and chief executive Garry Cook were prepared to give Hughes a chance, but by the summer of 2009, they were already eyeing up possible alternatives should he not make the grade. Mourinho was one, Mancini another. When Hughes began the season with five wins from the first six games, the only defeat being an unlucky last-minute 4–3 defeat in the derby at Old Trafford, it appeared that the under-pressure manager was turning things around. But the good start fizzled out, and after a run of seven straight draws, including home stalemates with lowly Fulham, Burnley and Hull, Sheikh Mansour ran out of tolerance. Khaldoon met with Mancini in London at the end of November to set wheels in motion, and a hapless 3–0 defeat at Tottenham on December 16, which made it one win from ten, was the catalyst for change.

That change was badly handled. The City hierarchy had decided to wait until after the home game with Sunderland on December 19 to announce Hughes's sacking and Mancini's appointment. But the news leaked out in Italy, and by the time the Blues kicked off, everyone in the stadium – including Hughes and his coaching staff – knew he was a goner. City won the match 4–3, and Hughes said his goodbyes at the final whistle, publicly humiliated.

Two days later, Mancini was presented to the media and promptly revealed that he had met chairman Khaldoon two weeks earlier: "I am sorry for Mark, but when you start these jobs, this kind of situation is always possible. I know the chairman from two weeks ago. He's a fantastic man. We met to discuss this situation, to speak on football. He wanted to know about what I felt about Manchester City. In Italy this kind of thing is normal. It's normal for people in football to do this."

Cook had to explain that the earlier meeting in London had been to sound out a possible replacement, and that real negotiation with Mancini had only begun in the aftermath of the White Hart Lane debacle. Increasingly irate, Cook thumped the table and said of the initial meeting: "The discussions were general, they were about football. We were considering our managerial options at that time. After the Spurs game, there were further discussions on a more serious level."

The embarrassment was palpable, and Mancini's career in English football management was off to an inauspicious start through no fault of his own. City fans were largely happy with the fact that Hughes had gone, but embarrassed by the cack-handed way in which the transition had occurred, and they were unsure about Mancini's pedigree – despite an impressive Italian CV he had no proven track record in English football, like Mourinho, nor the vast experience of Guus Hiddink, also considered for the post. Mancini had to earn the respect of the fans and of his players, and the only way to do that would be by winning matches and showing signs of real progress.

Brian Kidd, who had been appointed to a coaching post at the City academy three months earlier, was made assistant manager. It was a smart move – Kidd was born a few hundred yards from the stadium, and was an experienced and respected coach who had played a major part in Manchester United's successes in the 1990s, not least through scouting contacts that had helped to find and develop a generation of young stars. Mancini also brought over Fausto Salsano as a coach and Massimo Battara as goalkeeping coach.

The new manager declared that his aim was to try to secure a Champions League place at the end of the season, while a cup

Above: A young Roberto Mancini (front row, second right, wearing number 9) quickly showed star quality while playing for his home-town team during the 1970s.

Below: Mancini was only 16 years old when he got his first taste of top-flight Italian football, playing for Bologna in the early 1980s. He soon became the star of the team.

Above: Mancini (front row, second left) joined Sampdoria in 1982 and stayed at the club for 15 years. Trevor Francis and Liam Brady (back row, centre) were also there.

Below: England international David Platt also played with Mancini at Sampdoria. They became room-mates and friends, before joining up again at Manchester City.

Above: Having retired from playing, Mancini cut his teeth as an assistant to Sven-Goran Eriksson (right) at Roman side Lazio in 2000. The Swede was a major influence on Mancini.

Above: Mancini restarted his playing career with an unlikely move to Leicester City in 2001. Although his stay was a short one, it gave him a clear insight into English football.

Left: After returning to Italy, Mancini proved himself as a coach at Inter with three successive Serie A titles. Here, he embraces goalkeeper Julio Cesar after the second win in 2007.

Below: Installed as the new Manchester City manager in 2009, Mancini walked into a storm caused by the sacking of predecessor Mark Hughes, but soon won over the City fans.

Above: Mancini had already managed the mercurial Mario Balotelli at Inter before bringing him to City in 2010. Their relationship has been more father-son than manager-player.

Right: Carlos Tevez was already at City when Mancini became manager. The pair rowed over Tevez's apparent refusal to come on as a substitute during a Champions League match against Bayern Munich in 2011.

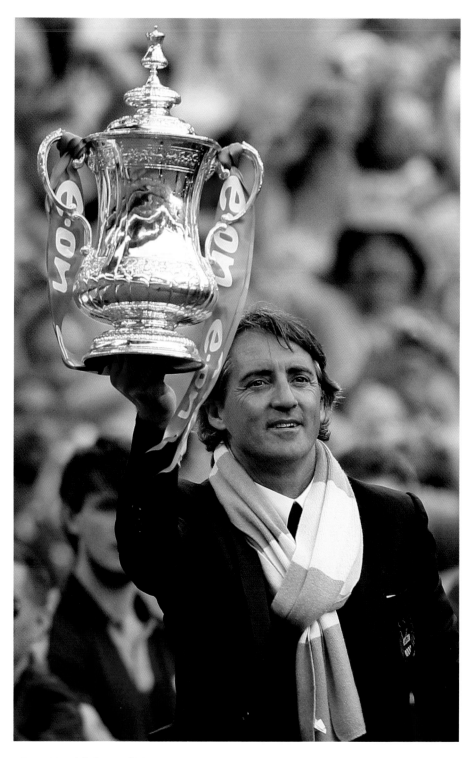

Above: Mancini shows off the FA Cup at Wembley after his team had ended the Blues' 35-year trophy drought, by beating Stoke City 1–0 in the final in May 2011.

Above: Mancini and triumphant City skipper Vincent Kompany soak up the adulation of the Blue masses as they parade the Premier League trophy around Manchester in May 2012.

would be a bonus. He would then seek to make an assault on the Premier League title in his first full season. He began well enough, the Blues looking well organized and efficient in his debut match, a 2–0 win over Stoke on Boxing Day 2009 with goals from Martin Petrov and Tevez. If he had any doubts about the importance of the squat, explosive Tevez to his new team, they were quickly dispelled as the Argentine striker scored twice in a 3–0 win at freezing Wolverhampton – their first away win for four months – and a hat-trick in a 4–1 home demolition of Blackburn.

The suave Italian also began a new trend at City, topping off his Giorgio Armani suit and immaculate overcoat with a cashmere City scarf tied in a stylish Windsor knot. It was a debut which pleased City's merchandisers, as it sparked a rush of scarf sales to copycat fans. The new man about town moved into a city centre hotel and would regularly be seen, along with Salsano and Battara, at one of the two swish Italian restaurants on King Street. City's new Italians gave the congregation at St John's RC Church in the Manchester suburb of Chorlton a surprise by turning up for a Christmas Eve mass – that congregation had once included the great Manchester United manager and Manchester City player Sir Matt Busby.

The Blues' new style icon would be given money to spend in the summer, but his first transfer window saw 34-year-old Patrick Vieira arrive on a free from Inter and promising young winger Adam Johnson, a deal already mooted before Mancini's arrival, snapped up for £7 million from Middlesbrough. The new boss made it plain that he had no favourites, drafting in out-of-favour players Martin Petrov and Javier Garrido, and handing debuts to three young players in his first month in charge.

One criticism of Hughes had been that he was not giving youth a chance as he strove for success, and part of Mancini's brief on taking over was to restore the Blues' long-standing reputation as a club which brings young players through. The new owners were prepared to spend big in order to compete with neighbours United, Chelsea and Arsenal, but they also paid close attention to the youth academy set-up, based on Platt Lane close to their old Maine Road ground. City fans are proud of the club's tradition of bringing through good young players, and Sheikh Mansour wanted to enhance that tradition by modelling City along Barcelona lines, and eventually producing their own superstars, rather than be forced to buy them in.

Hughes's reluctance to entrust his job to untested kids was understandable, to an extent. He felt that to compete at the sharp end of the Premier League, you need seasoned, reliable professionals, and cannot take risks with kids. In his 18 months in charge, Hughes handed a debut to just one product of City's academy, giving Vladimir Weiss the last 20 minutes of the meaningless last game of the season against Bolton. He had not followed the familiar route of using the cup competitions to introduce youngsters to the big time, as he was under pressure to lift the City hoodoo of not having won a trophy since 1976. In Mancini's first 18 months in charge, he gave debuts to 11 academy products.

Mancini knew he was expected to improve on Hughes's record on youth players, but he also had no qualms about putting his faith in the fearlessness of youth. He had made his own Serie A debut at 16 and as Inter coach had thrust 17-year-old Mario Balotelli into the heat of the title chase. He is a firm believer in the old football adage that if they are good enough, they are old enough. Within a month of taking over, he had given debuts to Abdi Ibrahim and Greg

Cunningham and even picked 19-year-old defender Dedryck Boyata to take on Wayne Rooney in both legs of the Carling Cup semi-final against Manchester United.

Those two derby games, Mancini's first big tests as City manager, came in the first five weeks of his reign, as Hughes had already guided the Blues into the semi-finals. Mancini vowed to tear down the hated Stretford End banner, but said that derbies were only important to fans – to managers and players they represented a chance to win three points or close in on a trophy. "I played in derbies in Genoa, Rome and Milan," he said. "The Manchester derby is the same as those in Rome and Genoa. The Milan derby is different. It is normal for fans to talk about the derby all year, but big clubs think about big situations and trophies. This game and the second leg are important for us because if we win we will go to Wembley. All fans think about derbies, which are one game, two games. But we must think about trophies and the Premier League."

The first leg, to be held at the City of Manchester Stadium, was postponed after heavy snowfall, but in the meantime Mancini made his first signing. Faced with a group of players he hardly knew, Mancini wanted someone in the dressing-room who would act as a lieutenant, in the way he been for Eriksson at Sampdoria and Lazio. He spoke to Juan Sebastian Veron, but a mooted £7 million move from Estudiantes came to nothing, so Mancini turned to 33-year-old Patrick Vieira, coming to the end of his playing days but still highly influential at Inter. "Patrick for me is a big player, an important player," said Mancini. "He won a lot of trophies with Arsenal, with Juventus, and with Inter, and I think he must continue at City. He can help us to improve our performance, for sure."

Vieira arrived at City with an injury which ruled him out of the
semi-final games against United, adding to the chorus of sneers
from critics who felt that Mancini, with vast wealth at his disposal,
had brought in an old crock on a free transfer to be his first
signing. They would eat their words as Vieira, despite only playing
28 games in his 18 months as a player for City, went on to play a
big part in their successes as an experienced dressing-room voice,
a confidant for younger players and an insightful contributor.
The French star said from day one that Mancini would be a
success for the Blues: "He will adapt himself really quickly, I'm
sure about that. He's somebody who likes his teams to go forward
and score goals. I think he will also bring added discipline to
the team. The game is the same wherever you are. You need to
be professional. You need to be disciplined throughout the 90
minutes and you have to prepare well. That has helped me to be a
better player."

Mancini had set about making City harder to beat, but it was
the strikers who were worrying him just days into his new job. With
Bellamy unhappy with his new manager, Roque Santa Cruz almost
a permanent fixture in the treatment room, Emmanuel Adebayor on
international duty and Benjani simply not up to the task, the Italian
had hoped to get a little more out of the world-class Robinho than
Hughes had. In his first season the Brazilian had been occasionally
brilliant at home but frustratingly anonymous away, and had then
suffered a stress fracture of his ankle which had kept him sidelined
since August. When he did play, there were no signs of trying to
impress the new manager – his attitude was poor and work-rate non-
existent, and Mancini had no patience for someone so uninterested,
British record signing or not.

With Tevez and the unhappy Bellamy carrying the flag, there was frightening news from Africa. The Blues' striker Emmanuel Adebayor, in Angola for the African Nations Cup, had narrowly escaped death when the Togo team bus was attacked by terrorists. Mancini was sympathetic, allowing the player, who had cradled a dying friend during the harrowing ordeal, to spend some time with his family in his homeland.

Mancini tasted defeat for the first time as City manager when he lost 2–0 at Everton on January 16. Robinho was sent on as an early substitute for the injured Santa Cruz, and hauled off an hour later after a display of supreme lethargy. Within a fortnight he would score in his final City appearance, an FA Cup win at Scunthorpe United, and then depart on loan to Santos, never to return to Manchester.

Tevez helped to ease Mancini into his new job by performing brilliantly, and he also gave the new boss his first derby victory by scoring both goals in the 2–1 win in the first leg of the Carling Cup semi-final. Tevez played like a man possessed, so determined was he to make his former United manager Sir Alex Ferguson, who had not regularly picked him for the Reds and then questioned the size of City's fee, pay for his disrespect.

When he scored, Tevez cupped his ears in a gesture aimed at Ferguson, and signalled to United substitute Gary Neville, as he warmed up, to keep his mouth closed – the defender had also questioned Tevez's worth. Mancini was outwardly unmoved by Tevez's actions, urging him simply to focus on his game in the second leg. No doubt he was smiling inside, realizing he had a player on his hands with the same fire and drive, and rage against the critics, which had helped to make him a special player. Tevez scored again in the second leg, but United won 3–1, continuing their habit of scoring last-minute goals in Manchester derbies, and Mancini's honeymoon period was over.

His first transfer window was also nearly over, and after picking up Vieira, City completed the signing of Johnson, whom he likened to a young Ryan Giggs. Attempts to take Real Madrid midfielder Fernando Gago fell through, and a deal for Parma midfielder McDonald Mariga fell foul of UK work permit regulations. Mancini would have to chase a top four place with no big-money reinforcements, and with one striker less, as he off-loaded Benjani to Sunderland.

The fact that Mancini had not moved his wife and daughter Camilla to Manchester – his two sons were pursuing their own football careers in Italy – was a sign that both manager and club were waiting to see how his appointment went before it became permanent. His contract was for three years, but the fact that Mancini was not about to put down roots straight away suggested he, and possibly the club, saw the first six months as something of a trial period. Doubts were already being raised in early February as fans picked over the carcass of a 2–1 league defeat at Hull City, their second in three games, and the cup defeat by United.

There was also trouble brewing off the field. Mancini saw his priority as shoring up a leaky City defence, and imposing his own disciplined team shape on the side, and he wanted things done his way. That would mean stepping up the training regime including double sessions at times, which would inevitably lead to friction, with some players already annoyed by his habit of changing the times of training sessions at short notice.

Hughes's sacking had been a shock for the City squad, especially for the fiery, opinionated Craig Bellamy, who had been the team's best striker in the opening months of the season and who had also served Hughes at Blackburn and played alongside him for the Welsh national team. He reacted angrily to the news of his old team-mate's sacking, decrying the lack of loyalty in the game and hinting that he was considering a future away from City. And within weeks of the new manager starting, he and Mancini had clashed over the best way to manage the 30-year-old's persistent knee problems. Hughes had allowed Bellamy leeway in training, but Mancini took a harder line and insisted he train with the main group at all times. Bellamy later said of the new regime: "It was a totally different structure which affected me completely. Mancini told me to stay with the team all the time. We had longer training sessions, but with no intensity whatsoever. He seemed to know my knee better than I knew it myself. He tried to explain why I had problems with it and what I should do about it. When I told him my knee was hurting, he tried to tell me it wasn't."

The two men argued, Bellamy was sent home, and their relationship started on a slippery slope which saw the player gradually relegated to the margins of the team, sent on loan to Cardiff the following season, and eventually allowed to leave on a free transfer to Liverpool.

An apparent coldness towards injured or unavailable players is a recurring theme in Mancini's management style. Wayne Bridge, another player who would find little sympathy as his form suffered and his career at the club slid into oblivion, said of Mancini: "He hates injured players – he will be like: 'No, they should be out training, it's not that bad.'" And when powerful defender Micah Richards was forced off the field with an injury in 2011, a reporter's query about his well-being was met with a joke: "He is Swarovski, like crystal," said Mancini, making it plain he had little time to worry about trivial knocks.

Bellamy had not been alone in voicing his discontent with Mancini's methods in the first weeks of his appointment, and as criticism mounted the manager made his position plain. As a player he had been a notorious moaner himself, he said, and it was part of a top player's make-up to question and challenge: "I can speak with my players when we don't have the same ideas about things, it is normal, and not a serious problem for me. I also read that the players are angry because I changed the time of the training sessions, and because we did more tactics. I read these things, but these are players, and for players, going onto the training ground and work on tactics, power and running are all normal. I understand that they don't have the habit of working on tactical situations, but I work with this method. If you want to win the Premier League and the Champions League, you must be prepared very well for every situation. The players have worked very well on the pitch, and it is incredible when I read that I have a problem with some players.

"I changed the time of training sessions because at 11 o'clock it was too cold and the pitches were frozen, which, for me, is normal. I believe I have the full respect and confidence of the players, and I always have respect for them. But when I work, I want to work well, and work to win. I don't work only because I enjoy playing football. If we want to win we must change our mentality, which also means thinking when we work. I have no problems with the players, apart from the normal ones that every manager has with his team."

Mancini received strong backing from one of his former players. Javier Zanetti, the Inter stalwart who had played in all but one of the 114 league games in the three title-winning seasons, said:

"Roberto Mancini is a big coach with the same characteristics as José Mourinho and Carlo Ancelotti. Like them he demands total responsibility from his players and high intensity levels during training sessions. You must offer total commitment and obey his orders or you will not be in the squad. Manchester City will find he loves the technical side of the game but also loves to attack."

But in February of 2010, Mancini was concerned about his team's flagging form in the absence of Tevez, who was in Argentina on compassionate leave after the premature birth of his second daughter. The response to adversity would be familiar to fans of Mancini's previous clubs, as he led City on a run of one league defeat in 11, even though they crashed out of the FA Cup to Stoke in that spell. In the middle of that run, Mancini would face his first league clash with one of the top four whose hegemony he was trying to smash. City went to leaders Chelsea in a match overshadowed by bad blood between the London club's captain John Terry and his England colleague and former neighbour Wayne Bridge, after it was revealed that Terry had an affair with Bridge's ex-girlfriend Vanessa Parroncel. Bridge refused Terry's offer of the customary "friendship" handshake before the game and City, some of whose stars had worn T-shirts in support of their team-mate in an earlier game, responded with a stunning 4–2 win with two goals each from Tevez and Bellamy.

That win prompted Mancini to begin planning for the long haul, and he started house-hunting. Until then his wife and daughter, and the families of the other Italians on his coaching staff, had stayed at home in Italy while the manager worked 18-hour days to try to knock City into shape.

Mancini also delivered a riposte to another unhappy player.
England winger Shaun Wright-Phillips had failed to impress in
Mancini's first weeks in charge, but was asking for a pay rise backed
up by his dad, former Arsenal striker Ian Wright, who claimed his
boy had been "mugged off" by City. Mancini suggested the player
should try to earn a new deal through his performances rather than
any media campaign: "If a player speaks with me it's much better for
the club. For example, I have no problem with Shaun, but it's always
in the newspapers that there are problems."

Italian observers had been surprised at just how serene Mancini
had become since joining City, at least in public – biting his
lip about refereeing decisions, politely admonishing errant
players, and showing nothing but respect for rival managers. That
changed when City's unbeaten run was ended by Everton, against
whom Mancini's own playing career had terminated. Everton
boss David Moyes had been an outspoken critic of City since
Hughes had plucked defender Joleon Lescott from his team in a
£22 million deal. Ahead of the game, he derided the Blues as a
team of individuals, and when he caught the ball, in added time
with his team leading 2–0, Mancini thought he was trying to waste
time. The City manager barged into Moyes to try to retrieve the
ball, there was a scuffle, and both men were sent to the stands.
Tempers soon cooled, Mancini apologized, and the managers
shared a drink after the match. But it was the first public sign
of the fires burning inside and earned Mancini his first FA improper
conduct charge and a £20,000 fine suspended until the end of
the season.

Mancio was also coming under fire from fans and media for being
too defence-minded at a club that had always prided itself on fielding

adventurous teams. That charge was partially answered by 14 goals in the next three games, a sneak preview of the free-scoring team which would sweep to the title two years later. Wigan were dispatched 3–0, Burnley were hammered 6–1 in a torrential downpour at Turf Moor, and Birmingham were dismissed 5–1 as City revved up for the derby by moving into fourth place with six games to go.

United were not ready to cede power to the Blues, famously dismissed by manager Sir Alex Ferguson as "noisy neighbours". The Reds left east Manchester with three points, through Paul Scholes's late winner, to set up an English record 19th league title and dump City back into fifth place. Mancini's first season now boiled down to a straight fight with Tottenham for the fourth place he had targeted from the start, the prize being a place in the Champions League which he felt would push the team, and the club, onto the next level.

After a draw at Arsenal and a win over Aston Villa, it was in City's own hands, with Spurs the visitors to Eastlands in the penultimate game of the season. Victory in that game, and on the last day at lowly West Ham, would secure Mancini's objective. But misfortune had struck at Arsenal when first-choice goalkeeper Shay Given dislocated his shoulder. Number two Joe Hart was at Birmingham on loan for a season and back-ups Stuart Taylor and David Gonzalez were recovering from injuries. Faroe Islands international Gunnar Nielsen had made his debut as a replacement for Given at the Emirates Stadium, but Mancini remained unsure about the untried 23-year-old. City tried to recall Hart, who had been Birmingham's player of the year, but ran into obstruction from the Midlands club, and in the end had to take Sunderland reserve Marton Fulop on an emergency loan.

Mancini entered the fight for fourth unsure whether he would be kept on by City's ambitious owners if he were to fail. "I think all managers need time," he said. "In Italy, if you don't do a good job in the first six months or one year, it's difficult because they sack all the managers every six months. Here it's different. I think at Manchester City it's different. I want to stay here 200 per cent and if the owners want me to stay, I will stay here. When you want to build a good team you must have time. I didn't buy players, I didn't build this team."

In the crucial match, Fulop palmed a cross straight to Spurs striker Peter Crouch, and Tottenham celebrated their first qualification for the Champions League in front of the disconsolate City fans. Mancini may have been "kissed by fortune" in Italy, but he appeared to have got a good kicking from Fate after moving to England – with key players going on compassionate leave, serious injury problems at important moments, and a hundred off-field distractions.

Those factors were recognized by the owner and chairman, who stressed that continuity was needed to drive City into the European elite. They had said something similar about Hughes, but the difference was that Mancini was their appointment, not an inherited manager, and they were prepared to stand by their own judgment.

Once the dust of defeat by Spurs had settled, the urbane, eloquent Khaldoon issued this statement: "Roberto is our manager and I think he has done an excellent job, coming in here mid-season and organizing the team. I'm very happy with Roberto and Sheikh Mansour is delighted with him. I believe that Roberto is going to do a wonderful job for many years. That's absolutely why we brought him to the club. I have the highest regard and respect for Roberto. He is a man who is driven, committed and who has a winning mentality. He wants to win and he wants to do things and achieve things for the club. He is definitely the right manager for this club for many years. I think that what he needs this summer is time to prepare. I'm really excited about next season already. I had a meeting last week and we are already in second gear in our preparations for next year. We have to move on and focus on the future, prepare and give Roberto all the tools he needs in order to be well prepared for next season."

Chapter Seven
Breaking the Spell

A stranger in a strange land, Roberto Mancini's first six months as an English football manager had been tough. He had walked into a storm over the sacking of Mark Hughes, had to weather the uncertainty and occasional hostility of some of the players he had inherited, and wrestled with expectation, fan impatience and the English language in equal measure. In the summer of 2010, after the endorsement of chairman Khaldoon al Mubarak and an extremely positive meeting in Abu Dhabi with owner Sheikh Mansour, he knew this was now his time. Not only had he received assurances about his own future, he had been told that he would be backed with money in what would turn out to be the most incredible summer in the history of Manchester City Football Club.

Along with chief executive Garry Cook and football administration officer Brian Marwood, Mancini had flown to Abu Dhabi, where he met Sheikh Mansour for the first time. Afterwards there were meetings with Khaldoon and fellow City director Simon Pearce, at which they put the finer points on their transfer strategy for the summer. Meanwhile Mancini had finally brought wife Federica and daughter Camilla over from Italy and settled in the smart Cheshire village of Alderley Edge.

With his position guaranteed, he could begin his work in earnest. Apart from bringing in Patrick Vieira, whose contribution in playing terms had been minimal because of injury, and Adam Johnson, Mancini had not been able to sign any players in the winter transfer window. He was forced to finish the season with what was to all intents and purposes Hughes's squad. Now City were about to embark on the biggest transfer spree in their history, as the owner backed the man he had appointed with unprecedented levels of cash.

Before the 2009–10 season was over, a deal was already in place to bring German international defender Jerome Boateng from Hamburg for £10.5 million, evidence that a priority for Mancini was to shore up his defence. The manager confirmed the deal to the *Manchester Evening News* after the Blues had wrapped up the season with a 1–1 draw at West Ham. "Boateng is a good player, a young player and strong," said Mancini. "He can play central defender, right defender, or in the middle, three different positions. If we find a player like that, who can play in two or three different positions, it is better for us. Next year we will play in four different competitions, which means playing every three days, so we need those players who can play in a few different positions."

The next move was to ensure that there would be no repetition of the goalkeeping crisis which had hit the club when Given injured himself at Arsenal in the closing weeks of the season. That meant recalling Joe Hart from a hugely successful season-long loan to Birmingham. Mancini's brief was to see to it that City had two top-quality players in every position, and he was intent on making sure that Given had some strong competition.

Chapter Seven

It was just the start. Before the end of the summer, City fans
would be open-mouthed at the quality of player coming in to
their club. Following Boateng's arrival, David Silva, Yaya Touré,
Mario Balotelli, Aleksandr Kolarov and James Milner would all
walk through the door for around £130 million, as the rest of the
Premier League stood back dumbfounded.

Mancini had watched his new team for five months and realized
that as well as having to change their football culture, and try to
transform the mentality which suffused the club, he also needed
a swathe of new, top-quality players to effect the transformation.
He made it plain that men like Stevie Ireland, Nedum Onuoha,
Benjani, Martin Petrov, Craig Bellamy and Emmanuel Adebayor,
although good players, lacked the mentality or the ability – or
both – for a team that aspired to be the best. He told the owners
what he needed, and then headed for his holiday villa in Porto
Cervo, Sardinia, to let the haggling begin. Identifying targets
is a meticulous process at City. Mancini made it plain that he
primarily wanted young players who would grow together as
a team, and who he believed would be more malleable and
receptive to his ideas. But he would also require a splash of big-
match experience.

Mancini felt City lacked the midfield spark they would need to
really take on United. Gareth Barry and Nigel de Jong had proved
to be solid, effective performers, but were a little one-paced, and
better defensively than they were going forward. Patrick Vieira
had failed to recapture the world-class form he had shown with
Arsenal, Juventus and Inter, and Stevie Ireland – the talented,
inventive midfielder who had come through the City ranks – had
gone backwards under Mancini. The midfield needed dynamism

and creativity, and Mancini had identified the men he wanted. In
the space of three days, at the height of the English summer, City
announced they had got their prime targets, paying £26 million for
Valencia's Spanish maestro David Silva and £24 million for Ivory
Coast international powerhouse Yaya Touré, from Barcelona.

Mancini had made a special study of attacking midfielders
when he took his coaching badges, and in Silva he had found his
trequartista. Yaya was a player who would keep play ticking and
link defence with attack, either through the economical possession
passing which is drilled into anyone who plays for Barcelona,
or through his penchant for quick, powerful surges which can
unhinge defences. Again, both men could fill multiple positions,
and Mancini was bursting with ideas about how to use them.

One City fan on a radio phone-in was less than enthralled
by the news that Yaya was one of the top summer targets: "Not
another bloomin' defensive midfielder" was his reaction. This was
an ungrateful response for the signing of a world-class player; and
it was also wide of the mark, a mistake which was to be repeated by
some sections of the media, long after it became apparent that Yaya
would be re-invented as an attacking player by Mancini.

Yaya had been an effective defensive midfielder at the Camp
Nou, and had even stood in as central defender as Barca beat
Manchester United in the 2009 Champions League final. But he
had made his name at Monaco as a thrusting, attacking player who
wedded immense physical power to deft touch and an impressive
range of passing. He would be described during his City days as
"a buffalo in ballerina shoes". Barcelona, blessed with the supreme
attacking talents of Xavi, Andres Iniesta and Lionel Messi, had
converted the muscular, 6ft 2in Ivory Coast international into an

anchor for the team. Mancini's decision to return him to his roots was a master-stroke.

There was no need to tinker with Silva's game. He was a small, perfectly balanced midfield genius with an exquisite touch; an instinctive passer with quick feet and an even quicker brain. Rejected when he was young by Real Madrid, who felt that he was too little ever to be a footballer, Silva had joined Valencia and proved that judgment abysmally wrong. However, there were many who felt that Madrid's original assessment might just prove right when he tried to transplant his abilities from the measured pace of La Liga to the more physical demands of the English Premier League.

The spending continued apace. Left back was another area of concern for City, a position which almost seemed cursed. Hughes had brought in England international Wayne Bridge, but he had proved to be defensively poor while the attacking abilities which had propelled him to stardom had waned. Hughes had also brought in former Arsenal man Sylvinho from Barcelona, a player whose professionalism and attitude greatly impressed Mancini but who was heading for retirement at the end of the season.

To fill the void, in mid July Mancini went back to one of his old clubs and picked up Lazio's Serbian international Aleksandar Kolarov in a deal worth £19 million. Kolarov was known for his powerful attacking runs and ferocious shot, especially from set-pieces – comparisons were even being made with Mancini's old team-mate Sinisa Mihajlovic, one of the best free kick and corner takers in football history. "I first saw Kolarov in his Lazio debut back in 2007," said Mancini. "I have watched him a lot since then and so have the Manchester City scouts. His attacking capability is very good. He is fast and can shoot with power and accuracy. He also has the ability to play in numerous positions and is very good in midfield. This is an additional benefit to the team. He has a fantastic international career ahead of him."

Mancini also wanted back-up for Tevez, who had carried the City attack that season scoring 29 goals, just one less than the other four strikers – Adebayor, Bellamy, Robinho and Santa Cruz – put together. Adebayor had gained weight and lost form in the aftermath of his terrorist ordeal in Angola, Bellamy's relationship with the manager remained uneasy at best, Robinho had vowed never to return to Manchester, and Santa Cruz had found his troublesome knee could not stand up to the rigours of a full English season. Benjani and Brazilian striker Jo had simply proved not good enough and had faded out of the picture.

The Blues were hot on the trail of Wolfsburg's Bosnian striker Edin Dzeko, who had just fired the unfashionable German side to their first Bundesliga title, but they faced stiff competition from Juventus, which was driving up the price. Mancini was also intent on testing Inter's determination to hold on to Mario Balotelli, whose precocious talent he had introduced into their first team at 17, and who had rewarded him with performances which belied his tender years. The young player had failed to see eye to eye with Mancini's Inter successor Mourinho, who deemed him "unmanageable".

But it was not all about bringing in expensive new players. Others had to be moved out, and some – Mancini felt – needed to take a hard look at themselves and decide whether they wanted to be part of this City revolution. The manager was not sparing in his opinions. He told Stevie Ireland that he needed to "change his head" if he wanted to be a top player, Mancini code for "shape up or ship out". The Irish midfielder had been player of the year under Hughes, but by the end of Mancini's first summer he had gone, sold to Aston Villa as part of the James Milner deal, complaining that he had never been given a chance.

The new boss said something similar about defender Micah Richards, a player who had exasperated successive managers by combining a powerful attacking capacity and supreme physical talents with the tendency to lose focus in defensive situations. Mancini's assessment was blunt: "He's played here for four or five years, and I think that he must improve. He has everything to do his job, but sometimes his concentration lets him down. Sometimes, his body is on the pitch, but his head is not." Richards took the words as a challenge, rather than an insult, and has gone on to be an important part of Mancini's squad, seeing off the challenge posed by the signing of Germany international Boateng.

Bellamy's card was marked in August, when he and Ireland were left out of the squad for the Europa League qualifying tie at Romanian side Timisoara. Mancini made his position clear by naming just 23 players when he was allowed, by Uefa rules, to submit 25. As if to rub it in, the manager included two men whose futures also looked to lie away from east Manchester, Santa Cruz and Robinho, as well as the untried Shaleum Logan and long-term crock Michael Johnson.

Bellamy had not impressed Mancini with his comments after the manager's bust-up with Moyes. The player now claimed, while on international duty with Wales in August, that Mancini was trying to force him out of the club, seemingly with some degree of justification. The final straw came when Mancini made it plain he would not be including Bellamy in his squad of 25 for the Premier League season, a clear pointer to the exit door. Just days into

the new season he left for a season's loan at his home-town
club Cardiff.

Mancini also wanted to see the back of young defender Nedum
Onuoha. At the end of the previous season the player had grown
increasingly disenchanted with his lack of first-team opportunities,
and his frustration culminated in an outburst on the Sky TV
Saturday morning show Soccer AM in which he had openly criticized
the new manager. In a frank interview, the big defender claimed that
Mancini did not like him, accused the manager of costing Joleon
Lescott a place in England's World Cup squad by mis-managing his
injury, and said he had snubbed "the best player at the club", Stevie
Ireland. Onuoha had made just six appearances in Mancini's half a
season in charge, and felt the writing was on the wall for his City
career. It certainly was after that interview, and he was farmed out on
loan to Sunderland when a permanent buyer could not be found.

Before the player shopping had been completed, there were
a couple of additions made to the coaching staff in that heady
summer of 2010 as Mancini staged a Sampdoria reunion on the
Carrington training pitches, bringing in old team-mates David Platt
and Attilio Lombardo. Former England star Platt, who had roomed
with Mancio in Italy, had walked away from football after quitting
as England under-21 manager in 2004, and had become managing
director of a golf business. When Mancini moved in next door but
one to Platt, who had already settled in the village of Alderley Edge,
it was almost inevitable that the two old room-mates would link up
again. When they were together at Sampdoria, Mancini respected
Platt as a player who would stand his ground. Mancio had wielded
extraordinary power at the club, but did not always get his way when
he disagreed with Platt. That struck a chord, and he took on Platt as

first-team coach. Lombardo had been a key element in Samp's 1991 Scudetto-winning side, and would bring "experience and a winning mentality" to the squad, the manager predicted.

Mancini had some news for those players who had grumbled about the double training sessions he introduced when he took over – it was about to get a whole lot harder as he prepared for his first full season in charge: "I think players here have a different culture from Italian players, but all players are the same," he said. "'They all want to play, they all want to win and they all don't want to work hard. I played for 20 years and I was the same. When I was young I didn't like to work either, but afterwards I realized you can win more if you work hard. For the first 15 days at City I think it was difficult because I changed training, though I didn't change everything. In the summer, though, I will change everything for the players. It will be difficult. I told them, 'Recover very well in the summer because, if we want to win next year, we will be working harder.'"

The way the manager viewed it, the real work on making City great began on July 6, 2010, when the first batch of players returned from their summer break. Many others would not return for several weeks owing to their World Cup commitments. Mancini had been parachuted into the club in mid season and asked to organize unfamiliar players, some of them hostile, into a side capable of challenging for a top four place. It had been a case of short-term remedies, patching up and making do. This was the moment he had been waiting for, when he could bring in some of his own choices, sideline those he felt were trouble, or simply not good enough, and then spend an intense 40 days drilling them into an outfit which really could change City's fortunes and win a trophy or two.

Mancini had himself been on a steep learning curve in his five months in charge. He had tried to learn English, even watching Coronation Street to familiarize himself with northern accents. He had also immersed himself in English football culture during his long stay in London a year earlier, but nothing can prepare you for taking a job in an alien culture. Mancini had been learning, in his spat with Bellamy, in the grumbles and groans on the training pitch – and off it – about the prevalent mind-set at Manchester City. Now he was determined to change it.

The challenge for the following season was obvious to Mancini, and had been starkly laid out by the owner, who had a bold four-year plan to take City to the Premier League title. His team had to remove the hoodoo of going 34 years without a trophy, and break into the top four – if possible, making a challenge for the Premier League title along the way.

"It's not my mentality to play for fourth position," said Mancini. "I don't think like this. I am very optimistic. This is going to be a good season for us. If the players follow me and trust me, if we all work really hard, we can change the history of this club. We are not worried about replacing Manchester United as the richest club in the world. We are building something for the future. This is normal, and other clubs have done it in the past, like United, like Chelsea. We want to be important and to win trophies. United are one of our rivals, but not the only one."

For the first time, he revealed that the desire to bring unprecedented success to under-achieving City was a large part of the appeal of the job, just as similar challenges at Sampdoria, Lazio, Fiorentina and Inter had fired his imagination. It was all about his love of being an underdog: "I always prefer to work to bring success to a club that hasn't won for many years. I spent my life at Sampdoria, who hadn't had much success. I played there for 15 years because I loved that club, and I wanted to win with them, and then I went to Lazio, who hadn't won the league for more than 20 years, and we won the title. At Inter, it was the same. At Fiorentina, they had not had much success, and I won the Italian Cup. For a player or a manager, it is an exciting challenge to try to make history at a club in this way."

So he set about his task in the summer of 2010 with relish, although he was frustrated by the fact that he did not have all of his new signings available in time for the start of pre-season training. Silva was delayed by his part in helping Spain to triumph in the World Cup final, and others who had taken part in the tournament were given much-needed holidays which ate into Mancini's precious preparation time.

His plans also had to be temporarily shelved when he was in Baltimore on the Blues' pre-season tour of the USA and he received a phone call from home – his dad Aldo had been rushed into the intensive care unit of a hospital in Ancona after suffering a heart attack, and there were fears for his life. Mancini left the squad in the hands of Kidd and Platt and caught the first flight to Italy, missing a 3–0 defeat by his former club Inter in a friendly. He returned to England once his dad was out of danger, ready to put the finishing touches to his new squad.

The City boss was gradually finding his feet and becoming more sure of his ground in English football, and felt moved to defend his club against accusations that they were buying success, which were accompanied by suggestions that the amount of money invested had piled pressure onto Mancini's shoulders: "Other teams are saying this because for ten years there were only four teams challenging for the title. All these teams over the years have spent a lot of money, not just us. Manchester United, Tottenham, Chelsea, Arsenal, Liverpool. They seem to have done like City do now. There isn't a difference."

The Manchester City argument is that spending big is a necessary ingredient in winning the major trophies, and that their spree only looked worse than others because it was crammed into a short space of time. That was the clear strategy of the owner, who wanted City competitive at the top of the Premier League in as short a space of time as possible.

Of course, having money also engenders jealousy and a desire to put one over on the nouveau riche upstarts of the Premier League, and no-one was more intent on slapping them back down than Tottenham Hotspur. They had already derailed Sheikh Mansour's plan with that crushing Crouch goal at the end of the preceding season, to snatch the final Champions League place. By a quirk of fate, the fixture list had pitted the two clubs against each other at White Hart Lane on the opening day of the season.

There was little doubt that Spurs were the team squarely in City's sights for that coming season. Mancini knew that his new team would need time to blend properly, and as a result it was extremely unlikely that they would be able to mount a serious challenge to neighbours United, Arsenal or champions Chelsea. Meanwhile Harry Redknapp's players were likewise under no illusions, as they too were ill-equipped to challenge for the crown, and knew that a scrap for fourth was probably as good as it would get in terms of the league.

The day before the start of the new season, City landed their fifth major signing of the summer with Mario Balotelli jetting into Manchester from Milan, too late to be included in the plans for the opening fixture at Tottenham. There were observers in Italy who felt that Mancini had taken leave of his senses, as Balotelli, who signed on his 20th birthday, had a growing reputation as trouble. But Mancini remembered his own days as the wild child of Italian football and believed that if he could guide the youngster in the right direction, tap into his footballing talents and keep him out of serious trouble, he would end up with a world-class striker.

"I think that Mario is one of the best players of his age in Europe, and I am very happy to be working with him again," said Mancini. "His style of play will suit the Premier League, and because he is still so young there is a big chance for him to improve. He is a strong and exciting player, and City fans will enjoy watching him. All of us are said to be bad boys when we are young, but I have worked with Mario before and he is a normal person. He is a young player, only 20 years old, who can do a lot in the Premier League. He has all the qualities needed to become a fantastic player."

There were fears that the pace of change was too quick, and that Mancini had ripped the heart out of the Blues by marginalizing players like Ireland, Bellamy and Onuoha. But the manager made it plain that he was developing a new, more solid, more durable spine to his team, and emphasized that it was a mainly English one: "In our squad we have Shay, Joe Hart, Wayne Bridge, Joleon Lescott, Gareth Barry, Michael Johnson, Shaun Wright-Phillips, Micah Richards. We need good players with strong characters. But we have nine, ten, eleven English players, and probably in the next week we will have four players who play for the national team. That's important. In every team in England it's important that they are together, stay together, speak in English. I think already I have five new fantastic players who will change our history. I think we have a chance to win the league. Why not? I have built my team and I hope it will not just be top four but better than that and we can win something."

That optimism would be put to the test at White Hart Lane the following day, and Mancini already had a big call to make. Given was the man in possession of the number one shirt, but now Hart had returned from his successful loan season at Birmingham and was not expecting to spend the campaign on the bench. Mancini had sent his trusted goalkeeping coach Massimo Battara to watch Hart during his loan spell at Birmingham, and the reports back had been positive. Mancini toyed with the idea of rotating goalkeepers, but it is a position which needs stability and continuity, along with the back four, if you are to build an understanding.

It was perhaps the biggest selection dilemma of his City career to date – having to choose between the seasoned veteran, just back to fitness after his shoulder injury at Arsenal in the previous season, or the thrusting young stopper, impatient to show he could nail down a permanent place both for City and for England.

Mancini plumped for Hart, and was rewarded in a big way. Tottenham put the Blues through a thorough examination on the opening day of the season, with debutant Kolarov given a torrid time before he was substituted at half time with an ankle injury. It was a rude awakening for Mancini, but he found some consolation in the fact that his decision to choose Hart had been spot on – the 23-year-old had a brilliant return to the City first team. He had not played for the Blues since Given had been signed in January 2009, when he had been dumped on the bench and then packed off to St Andrews on loan. The decision to play Hart brought another problem, as Given now made it plain that he too was not prepared to spend the season on the bench – his resolve to leave was heightened when Mancini again picked the young Englishman for the midweek Europa League game at Timisoara.

The Blues were in Romania for that game when the last piece of incoming transfer business took place, with James Milner heading for Manchester. He had played his last game, and scored, for Aston Villa on the first day of the season, and Mancini welcomed his addition to the squad in typically underwhelming style: "He is a good player and an English player, which is important. He can also play in different positions." Ireland departed for Villa Park as part of the deal, declaring he had also been "forced out" by Mancini. But the manager now had the requisite parts to make a challenge for honours, and had removed players who he felt were either disruptive or unnecessary.

After the draw at Spurs and a win at Timisoara – through Balotelli's goal on his debut – there was a real buzz around Eastlands for the Blues' first home game of the season, and not just because fans were anxious to see how the glut of glamorous new signings fared against Liverpool. In fact, injury to Balotelli, added to knocks for Boateng and Kolarov, meant that half of the new boys were not available.

The excitement was all because a rumour had rippled around Manchester that the club's owner Sheikh Mansour had finally turned up to see the team in action live, two years after he had taken control. The visit was hush-hush – Mancini and his players had not been told that their boss was in the house, and even some top brass at the club had only been told to expect "Garry Cook and Guest".

The welcome was rapturous, as grateful City fans clapped and chanted the owner's name, and the presence of the dapper, smiling figure in the directors' box inspired the team. Milner had a great debut, Tevez scored twice, and Roy Hodgson's Liverpool were dispatched 3–0. The manager was warmly greeted by the owner after the match, and the smiles spoke of a "project" that was on course to meet its objectives.

That project had begun two years earlier with the news that shocked European football, the £32.5 million signing of Robinho from Real Madrid. The week after Sheikh Mansour made his appearance at the stadium, the Brazilian finally departed, sold to AC Milan for £18 million. It was almost a signal that the evolution of the club had moved on to the next level. Robinho was bought as a statement, as well as in the hope that he would be an inspirational player. The former intention had been fulfilled, as the name of City had overnight become a serious player in the European transfer market, but as a player Robinho only left a few fleeting memories of quality. Mancini had no time for luxuries, or statements, he was in the serious business of building a winning team.

He was already caught in a dilemma. Despite the summer spending, he was still a long way short of having the size and quality of squad he felt he needed to compete at the top of English football, and make a foray into Europe. His dilemma was compounded by the fact that City's lack of success over the years meant that he could ill afford to neglect the lesser competitions. United, Chelsea and Arsenal all had Premier League titles tucked under their belts, as well as Champions League aspirations, so they could afford to be less than committed when it came to the domestic cup competitions. Their fans were accepting of the fact that they would use the cups to blood untried youngsters and give games to players on the fringe of the first team – in fact many of those supporters had come to enjoy the chance to look at the up-and-coming talent.

City were not in such a privileged position. Their last major trophy had been the League Cup in 1976, and many of their older supporters had grown up with a picture of Dennis Tueart's winning overhead kick in the final against Newcastle on their bedroom walls. Those fans wanted a trophy, any trophy, which meant that a manager who took the cup competitions lightly ran the risk of incurring their wrath, especially after the near miss when they had narrowly lost to United in the previous season's Carling Cup semi-final.

There was already pressure on Mancini when he took a seriously weakened team to play West Bromwich Albion at The Hawthorns on September 22. The bullish start to the season, and the feel-good factor surrounding Sheikh Mansour's visit, had already started to fade. Defeat at Sunderland, a poor display in a 1–1 home draw with Blackburn, and injuries to Balotelli, Boateng, Kolarov and Bridge, had invited the familiar pall of gloom to descend on Eastlands once more.

Silva had not so far had an impact, looking too lightweight for the greater demands of the Premier League, a waifish figure among the brutes who populate many an English midfield; and Mancini was moved to defend his prime summer signing, citing tiredness from his World Cup endeavours and subsequent international commitments: "He had just signed for us when he went off with his national team to play in Mexico. Then he came back and very quickly was off again with the national team again, this time to play in Argentina – another long trip. I thought he did very well when he came on against Blackburn, but I always said that he would need time because it is very different here than playing in Spain."

Yaya Touré had also not yet revealed his full repertoire, finding the pace of the English game difficult after playing on the Continent, while the injury troubles of Balotelli – who needed knee surgery – Boateng and Kolarov meant that five of the six new players had made minimal impact. Milner was the exception, but he was a seasoned Premier League campaigner.

Mancini laid it on the line to his players – the next six games, which consisted of league games against Wigan away and Chelsea and Newcastle at home, the Carling Cup tie at West Brom and the opening Europa League group fixtures against Salzburg and Juventus, would determine the course of their season. He also tackled fresh complaints from two of his stars head on. Given let it be known that he would seek to leave City in the January window, while Adebayor criticized the way his dead-leg injury was being managed. Mancini made it plain that the whinges had to stop: "We need a mentality like they have at Chelsea or United, where the players are used to winning trophies. I understand the players, because it is normal to be unhappy when you don't play. I don't find it frustrating as a manager, because I used to play football and behaved this way myself. I understand it, but it is important to change."

Wins in Salzburg and Wigan saw Mancini's targeted six-match streak off to a good start, but a defensive injury crisis landed the manager in a serious quandary for the Carling Cup game at The Hawthorns. The Blues were without Boateng, Bridge, Richards, Kolarov and Joleon Lescott, and less than 72 hours after the tie they faced a crunch match with leaders Chelsea, who had won their first five matches, scoring 21 goals and conceding one. It was a big call, but Mancini decided to wrap his front-line players in cotton wool – he handed debuts to youngsters John Guidetti, Ben Mee and Javan Vidal, and rare starts to three more kids, Greg Cunningham, Abdi Ibrahim and Dedryck Boyata. The back four was made up of two 19-

year-olds and two 21-year-olds, while the big guns were either on the bench or rested entirely.

West Brom took advantage in a 2–1 victory, and the four possible trophies had become three. City fans who made the trip to the Midlands were not impressed, but Mancini was unrepentant: "I don't regret making the changes. I have big problems at the moment and we couldn't take any risks. If I had more players available it would be a different team. But when you play like us and Chelsea, on Saturday at 12.45, the time to recover is very short. They would need a minimum three days, so to play them at West Brom would have been dangerous."

The gamble paid off as City ended Chelsea's winning streak, the defence demonstrating a new solidity to hold off Carlo Ancelotti's previously rampant attack and Tevez scoring a brilliant winner. Buoyed by the victory, City proceeded to beat Newcastle and win a 3–2 thriller at Blackpool, the match in which Silva suddenly sparked into life. The little Spaniard turned the game around from a 2–1 deficit with a sparkling performance, including a breathtaking individual goal.

The Blues were also easing towards qualification for the knockout stages of the Europa League after Adebayor shook off his disgruntlement and poor form with a hat-trick in the home game with Lech Poznan, but patchy form soon returned to haunt them again. Arsenal won 3–0 at Eastlands, Boyata having been red-carded after five minutes; the Blues lost in Poznan – an away trip which would spark a new dance craze among the fans; and then they slumped 2–1 at Wolves.

The slump was accentuated by the fact that four City stars – Hart, Johnson, Barry and Given – were caught on video at a drunken students' party during a golfing break in Scotland. Mancini, who had given his players some saucy advice – that it was "better to go with a woman than have a drink" – was unfazed by the footage. He shrugged off the incident, making the point that the four had not broken any club rules, but warned his players to go easy on the booze if they wanted to win trophies.

Balotelli got the Blues back on track by scoring his first league goals for the club in a 2–0 win at West Brom, but was also sent off for a petulant kick at Youssuf Mulumbu, which ruled him out of the Manchester derby three days later. That widely anticipated clash between second-placed Reds and fourth-placed Blues produced only a dull goalless draw as two cautious sides cancelled each other out. United were the happier, as the away team, and the stalemate meant that they had not been beaten by City in a league game since the takeover which had threatened to tilt the balance of power away from them.

When days later City again drew 0–0 against Birmingham City, the restlessness inside the stadium was tangible, and the critics labelled the Blues as simply too dull, too defensive – too Italian – to prosper in the Premier League. Mancini's decision to take off Tevez, who had been carrying a knock, and replace him with Barry, brought boos, causing him to hit back afterwards: "If you think I put four strikers on and we score four goals, it is not true. All supporters are like this, in England and Italy, but I must think like a manager. We can play wide, get the ball into the box, then we can score. Supporters just think, 'Why don't you put more strikers in the box – two, three, four, five?'"

The discontent was quietened as the Blues went to Fulham in their next game and put on a sublime display of attacking football against a side managed by former manager Hughes, with Diego Maradona watching from the Craven Cottage stands. Fittingly, Tevez scored twice and his fellow Argentine Pablo Zabaleta smashed in a screamer – and the City fans gleefully chanted, "Boring, boring City!" After the game, Mancini gave vent to his exasperated feelings towards those who continued to doubt the credentials of his team and himself: "Last week I was a stupid manager who was six points behind. Now, I am the 'best manager' because I am only three points off the top of the league. If we have a big problem and a big crisis and we are only three points behind United and Chelsea, then we are doing well."

He also suggested that any attempts to pile pressure on him at City were meaningless, after the time he spent in the San Siro goldfish bowl: "When you have worked for Inter Milan for four years it is impossible to be under pressure. They are one of the top teams in Italy and one of the biggest clubs in the world. When I went there, they hadn't won anything for 25 years. I was under pressure every day with people demanding to know, 'When will Inter win? When, when, when?' But I stayed four years, which is a big record for a manager there."

When the Blues were denied a win at Stoke through a last-minute equalizer, and then beat Bolton and West Ham with Yaya Touré scoring twice as he finally started to find his feet in the Premier League, they were left with an enticing prospect. A home win over Everton on December 20 would put them top of the table for the first time in Mancini's reign – and they were already through to the last 32 of the Europa League.

There was another problem looming on the horizon, with Tevez dropping the bombshell that he wanted to leave the club. The Tevez saga, and Mancini's handling of Mario Balotelli will be dealt with in detail in Chapter Nine, but it briefly cast a pall over the Blues as they prepared for an assault on the top four, the Europa League and the FA Cup in 2011.

Tevez withdrew his transfer request ahead of the Everton game, but the Blues slumped to a 2–1 defeat against their bogey team, and had to spend Christmas in familiar mode gazing up at neighbours United, who were sitting on top of the tree. The problem was clear to Mancini – his team was now more difficult to beat, but needed more goals and was over-reliant on Tevez to get them. By the time they won 3–1 at Newcastle on Boxing Day, a victory which marked the anniversary of Mancini's first game in charge, the Argentine striker had bagged ten league goals while Balotelli had been plagued by injury, suspension and immaturity and Adebayor had made it plain he did not want to be at the club.

Mancini had harboured hopes that he could revive the City career of Jo, the tall Brazilian striker who had signed for City in the summer of 2008 in a deal worth a club record £18 million but had been a major flop. Mancini remembered him giving his Inter team a hard time in the Champions League in 2007–08. But Jo had simply not settled at City and was not the answer to Mancini's problem.

The interest in Dzeko had never gone away. The 6ft 3in striker had been a revelation as Wolfsburg won the Bundesliga title in 2009–10, finishing as top scorer and drawing in scouts from all of Europe's top clubs. City had been among them and even when their bid to sign him had failed in the summer, they retained their interest and had not lost contact with Wolfsburg. Bringing in the big Bosnian in a mid-season transfer window was not ideal, especially for Mancini, who sets great store by working with his players in pre-season.

In this case, however, there was no real alternative. Reinforcements were badly needed, especially as the manager wanted Adebayor out of the way. The Togolese striker had made just two league starts in the first half of the season, and had appeared uninterested and half-hearted. With Real Madrid showing an interest in taking him on loan, Mancini was happy to get him out of the camp.

The imminent arrival of Dzeko seemed to fire Balotelli into action. The youngster had struggled to come to terms with the physical nature of the Premier League, was homesick and had started to earn himself a wacky reputation off the field. But against Aston Villa, just days before Dzeko's signing was announced, he fired in a quality hat-trick to remind everyone he had been signed for his footballing talent rather than his novelty value. That 4–0 win meant Mancini had his first taste of life at the top of the Premier League, albeit a brief one; a few hours later United's draw at Birmingham saw them regain the lead on goal difference.

But Mancini got his man early in the transfer window and was convinced that Dzeko's arrival, if he settled quickly enough, could yet give his side the right blend, and the impetus, to challenge for the title. "I think he'll be a very important player for the future of this club," said the manager. "We wanted him in the summer because we knew he was the perfect player for us. He is different from the other players we have. Now we have a good mix."

Chapter Eight
Silver Moon

Exactly ten years after they both walked out of Lazio, Roberto Mancini and Sven-Goran Eriksson were side by side on the touchline again … this time as rivals. By a strange quirk of fate, Mancini's City had drawn Eriksson's Leicester City as their first opponents in the FA Cup, a third-round tie which was rich in connections with the past. It would also prove to be the start of Mancini's future success as City manager, as it launched the Blues – rather unconvincingly – on the road to Wembley and the end of a 35-year trophy hoodoo.

Eriksson, of course, not only had strong personal connections with his former protégé Mancini, but was a former Manchester City manager himself, and one whose anticipated sacking in the spring of 2008 had provoked a "Save Our Sven" campaign in Manchester. Meanwhile Mancini had a powerful connection with Leicester, the club with whom he had finished his playing days.

And for the City fans in the crowd, it was an emotional day. The team wore specially commissioned red-and-black striped shirts in honour of former striker Neil Young, who had worn those colours as the scorer of the only goal when the two teams met in the 1969 FA Cup final. That had been the last time City had won the competition, and Young, who was dying of cancer, had been admitted to hospital on the eve of the match. Mancini donned a red-and-black bar scarf to go with his lucky blue-and-white one on a day for poignant memories for both managers, and for everyone connected with City.

The fact that a day so heavy with thoughts of things past should herald the start of City's bright new future was entirely appropriate.

Mancini was not faced by an injury crisis like the one which had led him to field a severely weakened side in the Carling Cup tie at West Brom. He was also aware that unless his team could find another gear in the league, they would be relying on the FA Cup to sate the club's desperate hunger for silverware. He had Balotelli and Silva injured, and rested Yaya Touré, Gareth Barry and Vincent Kompany, but the team was still packed with internationals. They survived a scare at the hands of Eriksson's feisty Championship side, coming from behind to lead through goals from Milner and Tevez before Hart's uncharacteristic handling error handed Leicester an equalizer.

The popular opinion of Mancini's squad, as the old year had turned into new, was that it was something of a shambles. Tevez was unhappy and had handed in a transfer request, only to withdraw it again eight days later; Balotelli was homesick, injured and had been pictured fighting with team-mate Jerome Boateng on the training ground; players were grumbling and griping; and just days into the new year Kolo Touré and Emmanuel Adebayor had a bout of fisticuffs in another bust-up on the Carrington practice pitches. The team was also bottom of the Fair Play League, which reflects the number of red and yellow cards received, and fouls committed, and was roundly criticized for being too defensive, especially after a backs-to-the-wall goalless draw at Arsenal early in January.

When questioned about the scrap between Adebayor and Kolo Touré, Mancini laughed it off as a natural consequence of the fact that a public footpath ran past the perimeter of City's training ground, and the council's refusal of planning permission for a high fence. That meant City's stars were visible to the paparazzi who patrol the perimeter on a virtually daily basis, and the kind of training-ground fights which happen at every football club, especially when places in the team are at a premium, are on show to the world.

Mancini rode it all with resigned good humour. This was no tempest – unlike the villainy, violence, unpaid players and refereeing scandals of his days in Italy, which had been true storms. This was a squall in an English teacup. "Sometimes we try it this way for them – to fight for them so they can take pictures!" he said. Then, in more serious mode, he added: "This happens in every team. The difference is that here we don't have a big wall. I played football and I know that in every team these things can happen when you train every day and play a match at 100 per cent. I am absolutely not bothered by this and like my players to be competitive on the training ground, as they are at every club."

As for his side being labelled "dirty" for its poor disciplinary record, Mancini was equally unmoved, and perhaps showed that his old suspicion of referees, which had been vindicated by events in Italy, had left scars: "The disciplinary table means nothing to us, and I would rather we are top of the Premier League, but I find it strange because we always try to play. I can't think why we should get so many yellow cards. I didn't agree with two of the five we got at Newcastle. And one thing I did notice is that we didn't get a clear penalty when Carlos Tevez was fouled. Every game we seem to get a penalty for which the ref doesn't whistle."

Chapter Eight

Mancini's wish to be top of the table that counts was briefly granted as the Blues edged a thrilling 4–3 win over Wolves, Dzeko making his debut. But the game showed some of the latent frailties in his team, as well as the blossoming attacking play. They switched off in the last ten minutes and were left clinging on in a game they had led 4–1. Mancini was not happy, warning his team that their failure to maintain concentration late in games would end up costing them in more vital situations later in the season.

Three days later, plucky Leicester were beaten 4–2 in the replay, and again Mancini was unhappy that his team made hard work of it, Tevez missing a penalty and his defence looking unsure in the face of a lively Championship side. But City were on the march in the FA Cup, and the ongoing tributes to the ailing hero of 1969, Neil Young, gave their progress an air of destiny.

It was just as well that City did rumble into the cup action, because after a splendid run of just one defeat in 17 matches in all competitions, serious inconsistency had them out of the title race by mid-March. After the seven-goal thriller against Wolves and the six-goal cup feast against Leicester, the Blues whimpered to a 1–0 defeat at Aston Villa, the goal scored by their debutant Darren Bent.

The Blues had continued to trim their squad, with Roque Santa Cruz going on loan to Blackburn while Adebayor was sent to Real Madrid until the end of the season, as Mancini put his faith in Tevez, Dzeko and Balotelli to score the goals which would get the team into the Champions League. Adebayor arrived in Madrid and claimed that Mancini had "lost confidence" in him. Former City star Gary Owen, writing in his *Manchester Evening News* column, sounded almost incredulous: "I never thought I would see the day. City have a £25 million player who can't get in the team, and Real Madrid come, cap in hand, asking if they can take him on loan!"

Adebayor's parting shot at Mancini was becoming commonplace at City. No-one was leaving with words of understanding and praise for the manager, and that was perhaps due to Mancini's practical, hard-line view of his job. That players feel disgruntled when they are not in the team is an age-old truth of football, and managers prefer their players to be fractious and angry when they don't get picked. Anyone who happily accepts a place on the bench, or in the stands, should be of more concern. Mancini himself was a frightening prospect for coaches who left him out – he has even suggested that he moved to get rid of Sampdoria coach Eugenio Borsellini in his anger at being named as substitute too many times.

With Mancini there is rarely a managerial arm around the shoulder for anyone not in the team. His attitude is that his door is open if a player has a problem, but he will not go out of his way to explain himself to anyone who does not get picked. His is a more Italian approach, where the relationship between player and coach is usually on a far more professional basis – in England there is more of a tradition of the father-figure manager, who involves himself in other aspects of a player's life. "When you're in, you're in, when you're out, you're nothing" is one City insider's take on Mancini's view. Injured players, suspended players, players out on loan – these do not exist in his mind, and he is sometimes unaware of the nature of an injury, unless it is a serious one.

As the January transfer window clanged shut, and Adebayor, Santa Cruz and Bridge headed out of the club and out of Mancini's thinking, City were well placed, six points behind leaders United in the league, in the last 32 of the Europa League and still in the FA

Cup having drawn 1–1 at League One side Notts County in the fourth round.

The trip to Meadow Lane was another game creaking with connections for the City manager – superstitious City fans with an eye for omens had started to reckon up all of these coincidences and come to the conclusion that their name might just already be written on the cup. Mancini had been invited to manage the Nottingham club in the summer of 2009, when Eriksson was sporting director. He had turned the job down, and the current incumbent was Paul Ince, an old Serie A adversary of Mancini from the Englishman's days at Inter.

In that clash between the world's oldest professional club and the world's wealthiest club, the Blues hardly looked like a side destined to lift the trophy at Wembley in May. In fact, a team which started with 11 internationals looked like being the embarrassment of the round as they trailed to Neal Bishop's goal until ten minutes from time. They were rescued by Micah Richards, who made a powerful run down the right and crossed for Dzeko to score his first City goal.

The Blues were without Adam Johnson for the game after he had damaged ankle ligaments during a typically feisty training session, and the lack of a wide option simply added to Mancini's frustrations with his developing team. Those frustrations doubled as the Blues twice threw away leads to draw 2–2 at Birmingham, days after the draw at Notts County. United were looking imperious at the top, having extended their unbeaten start to the season to 24 matches the night before the Blues slipped up at St Andrew's.

The more optimistic City fans had harboured hopes that their star-studded team might start to gel in the second half of the season, and that United's propensity for draws might just allow the Blues to stage a title challenge. But City's own inconsistency was costing them, and it had started to look as though they would have to fight to get into the top four, and hope that the FA Cup or Europa League might offer a chance of a trophy.

With some City fans again getting restless with the style of Mancini's team, the manager took the blame squarely on his own shoulders: "I am disappointed with myself because I am the manager and don't want my squad to play like this. I want them to play football. We have started to concede a lot of goals. We have been marking badly at set-pieces. It is impossible for a top team to defend like that."

Tevez relieved some of the pressure with a hat-trick which saw off West Brom, but next up was a do-or-die derby with United at Old Trafford. Victory for the Blues would cut the gap at the top to two points, as United had just suffered their first league defeat of the season at Wolves. But defeat would mean the Reds were eight points clear of City with a game in hand, and Arsenal would be the only realistic challengers.

The Saturday lunchtime showdown saw David Silva deflecting in an equalizer to Nani's first-half goal for United, but was settled by one of the great Premier League goals, as Wayne Rooney launched into a spectacular overhead kick. It was yet another crushing blow for Blues fans, who had seen their team lose five and draw one of the six league derbies they had played since the takeover. But for Mancini, the fact that his side had lost to an astonishing, unstoppable goal, after they had been the better team for long spells, was simply an encouragement. While the fans saw more misery, Mancini, unaffected by the century-old Manchester rivalry, saw only improvement.

A goalless draw away to Greek side Aris Salonika on February 15 set City up nicely in the Europa League, and saw the return of Balotelli, making his first appearance of 2011 after his knee problem. The Blues followed that by easing into the fifth round of the FA Cup with a 5–0 replay win over Notts County, another goal by Dzeko doing little to quieten his growing band of critics. The draw had been kind, as they landed a home tie with Aston Villa in the last 16.

Able to forget the problem of their flagging league form for a while, City secured their place in the last 16 of the Europa League as Dzeko – still without a league goal – scored twice in the home leg against Aris to set up an easy 3–0 victory and book a date with Dynamo Kiev in the next round. Dzeko was being harshly judged just a month into his City career, when he was clearly finding it hard to adapt, having been parachuted into the middle of an English season. But the criticism also reflected on Mancini, whose signings were being questioned. Silva and Yaya Touré had started to show exactly why they had been his prime choices to revitalize the Blues midfield, but Boateng had found it hard to nail down a place, Balotelli had suffered with injury and disciplinary problems, Kolarov had looked defensively uncertain and now the consummate Wolfsburg goalscorer Dzeko was finding it tough at City without a wide supply route.

Mancini needed a cup run to distract minds from indifferent league form, a situation which became more apparent when they were held 1–1 at home by Fulham as the league schedule resumed. Mark Hughes had managed Fulham to the draw, a stark reminder to Mancini that it was the kind of underwhelming result which had cost his predecessor his job. City's continuing defensive frailties had Mancini praying for a sequence of 1–0 wins, but his team had

responded to Balotelli's sharp opening goal by throwing away yet
another lead.

Mancini's frustration was palpable, and he clashed with Hughes at
the end of the game. The Fulham boss withdrew from the traditional
managers' handshake, accusing his opposite number of failing to
look him in the eye, and the two men exchanged unpleasantries.
Afterwards Mancini accused Hughes of similar disrespect when
the two teams had met at Craven Cottage earlier in the season: "In
London he did the same," said Mancini. "I know he said something
but I couldn't understand what. He should be happy his team got a
draw against us." Hughes countered: "I am old-fashioned. I always
think you should offer your hand in whatever circumstances, no
matter how difficult it is. I did it and did it with sincerity after my
team had been beaten 4–1 at Craven Cottage earlier in this season. I
acknowledged his team were better. Maybe I misread it, but I don't
feel Roberto really acknowledged the efforts of my team and what we
had done by the manner he offered his hand, by not looking at me."

Mancini's annoyance burst out in other ways, as he criticized
Balotelli, saying he needed to see more from him, and then publicly
questioned his medical staff over the slow recovery times of Nigel de
Jong, James Milner and Micah Richards. Balotelli at least appeared
to pay heed as he produced a top-quality finish in the FA Cup fifth-
round tie with Aston Villa to help the Blues to a comfortable 3–0
win – after which another kind draw, at home to Championship club
Reading, meant the chances of a semi-final place were very real.

But the growing cup fervour was dampened the following day
when it emerged that defender Kolo Touré had failed a drugs test
taken after the Manchester derby the previous month. The Ivorian
had taken one of his wife's water tablets after becoming obsessed with

his weight, and the random test had revealed a specified substance. He and Kompany had established themselves as City's first-choice centre backs, with Lescott finding it hard to produce the kind of form which had prompted the Blues to pay Everton big money. Indeed, there had been speculation that Lescott might be allowed to leave during the transfer window.

The sudden loss of Kolo meant that Lescott was pressed into action, and that proved to be a key moment in the history of the Blues. Mancini was forced to pair Kompany and Lescott – and, through the accident of Kolo's misfortune, hit on a combination which would underpin two trophy victories in the next 14 months.

Kompany himself had not been a regular in defence when Mancini walked into the job. In fact, under Hughes he had been used largely as a holding midfielder, the position he preferred to play. He had turned out in central defence a handful of times for Hughes, and had only just recovered from a toe injury when Mancini had taken over. In Mancini's first game in charge, he dropped Nedum Onuoha and pushed Kompany into the heart of his defence, and the Blues instantly looked more secure. The highly intelligent Belgian had a reputation in his home country of being a little difficult, but his conduct and professionalism at City have made a nonsense of that view, and he has – perhaps more than any other player – been the bedrock on which Mancini built his success.

At first Kompany hankered after his old position in midfield, but once he began to get rave reviews as a committed, hard-tackling, fiercely competitive and cultured centre half, he resigned himself to his fate and concentrated on becoming the best at his new position. When Kolo failed his drugs test in March 2011, Kompany found a new partner, and he and the left-footed Lescott struck up a symmetry and understanding which would become key to City's success. That was another stage in the evolution of the team, and with Silva and Yaya Touré starting to live up to their "world-class" billing, and Hart performing superbly in goal, the spine of the team was starting to look very good.

Silva's goal against Wigan was not quite world class, his tame shot trickling through the legs of keeper Ali al Habsi to give the Blues a 1–0 win as the club tried to absorb the shock of Kolo's suspension, pending an FA hearing. When United suffered successive defeats by Chelsea and Liverpool, hopes of a late title surge were briefly awakened, but Mancini privately knew his side did not have the solidity and consistency to maintain the kind of winning run needed to push them into pole position. The one-off nature of cup football, which had suited his spontaneous nature as a player in the Coppa Italia, was a different matter.

European hopes took a serious blow on a freezing night in the Ukraine as the Blues succumbed 2–0 to veteran star Andriy Shevchenko and his Dynamo Kiev side. Balotelli had been listless in the first half, and emerged for the second half holding his face. He was quickly substituted, the official explanation being that he had an allergy to the type of grass used in cold climates, and had suffered a reaction which had caused his face to swell. It was a disappointing night, but with the Blues arriving back in Manchester at 5am on Friday morning and due to play Reading in the fifth round of the FA Cup two days later, there was no time to dwell on it.

On paper, the tie with Reading looked straightforward, as they were a Championship outfit. But the fact that they had ousted Everton in the previous round by winning at Goodison Park proved they were no pushover. And when the draw for the semi-finals was made ahead of the Sunday afternoon game, and it pitted the winner against Manchester United at Wembley, suddenly the stakes were very high. On the night, the Blues looked flat and uninterested, and they were grateful to Micah Richards's towering header with 14 minutes left to book them a place in the last four and that monumental showdown with the old enemy.

Mancini was quick to point out that the last meeting of the clubs had been settled by an extraordinary Rooney goal, his way of suggesting that maybe the only difference between the two Manchester clubs was a moment of brilliance. "We have improved a lot in the last year and every time we have met United we have played at the same level," he said. "Maybe they have won a lot of trophies and have done that for a long time, but I feel we are very close and maybe next year we will be on the same level with United, Chelsea and Arsenal."

Derby fever enveloped Manchester, especially as this would be the first time the two clubs had ever met at Wembley. The match also appeared to take on new significance, with City still clearly on the rise and questions being asked about United's future, as manager Sir Alex Ferguson appeared to be shackled by the debts incurred by their 2005 takeover by the American Malcolm Glazer. City fans gleefully drew attention to the world of difference between the benevolent Sheikh Mansour takeover of their club and the leveraged buyout which had occurred across the city. The semi-final was viewed as a possible tipping point, the day when the balance of power in Manchester football, and English football, would finally tilt into the Blue after 35 years of rarely interrupted Red dominance.

By the time the semi-final was played, at teatime on Saturday April 16, the game was vitally important for City and possibly for

Mancini's future at the club. The Blues had gone out of the Europa League and then lost two out of three league games to slide 13 points behind United. Even fourth place was in jeopardy, as Tottenham had clambered to within three points with a game in hand.

The home leg against Dynamo had also raised more doubts about Balotelli's suitability, as he was red-carded for a reckless chest-high lunge at an opponent, leaving his ten team-mates to struggle manfully to a 1–0 victory which was not enough to overturn the deficit. With Dzeko also not coming to terms with life in England, Mancini's judgment of the two players was being called into question.

Three days later City lost 2–0 at Chelsea, with Balotelli banished from the team for his red card against Kiev, Tevez injured and Dzeko misfiring. So Mancini had plenty to ponder as he slipped out of Stamford Bridge on a motorcycle taxi in order to catch a flight back to Italy from Heathrow. The Blues boss was spending the first few days of the international break visiting family and checking up on the health of dad Aldo, on the mend after his heart attack the previous summer. The fortnight away from domestic action also gave some of his players a rest, and they looked more refreshed as they returned to action with a 5–0 thrashing of Sunderland at Eastlands.

There was just one more game before Manchester headed south for Wembley, a Monday night affair against Liverpool. City were now anxiously glancing over their shoulders at Tottenham, rather than seeking to close in on United at the top. All hope of closing the gap disappeared at Anfield, as the Blues suffered the heaviest away defeat of Mancini's time in charge, Andy Carroll scoring twice in a 3–0 defeat. To make matters much worse, Tevez limped out of the game with a hamstring tear which ruled him out of the semi-final, five days later.

The Blues were in bad shape. Mancini admitted he had made an error in preparing his team for the Liverpool game, and even appeared to suggest he had underestimated Kenny Dalglish's side. "I am disappointed with myself because I made a mistake. It was my fault – not the players'," he said. "It is important that I understand that it was my mistake. I made a mistake in the last two days but I know why. We probably thought that if we played this game less than 100 per cent we could still get a win. But football is not like that. I have learned something about myself. I have a lot of experience so it was my mistake, not the players'. I am sure we will get in the Champions League and we will get to the final."

Few Blues believed him, with Tevez out, which meant they would rely on the fragile character of Balotelli. Mancini chose the days before the big Wembley date to remind his team of the importance of what lay ahead, not just in terms of booking a place in the final: "All my players should understand very well this is a big moment for us. The first trophy is the hardest but it is time for Manchester City to win something."

Likewise few people thought Mancini would risk throwing Balotelli into the cauldron of a derby day at Wembley, with emotions seething, in what was one of the biggest days in City's history. Playing with just one striker, the safer option would have been to draft in Dzeko, but Mancini knew that "Super Mario" could rise to the occasion, give the United defence problems and possibly be a match-winner.

When the big day came, the manager's judgment on Balotelli looked perfect, as the Italian striker raised his game and led the line superbly. That was not the only call Mancini got right. Perhaps his bravest decision of the day came when, after reminding his players of their responsibilities, he walked out of the dressing-room in the minutes leading up to kick-off. He left his players to sort it out for themselves, led by stand-in captain Vincent Kompany. What was said in the dressing-room remains a secret, but it clearly helped, and it was a sure sign of Mancini's growing trust in the winning mentality of his own players. After the shambles at Anfield, the manager also got his preparation and tactics spot on – summer signing Yaya Touré was a dominant midfield force, and Mancini gave a sneak preview of his intentions for his team the following season with a tactical plan which involved pressing United high up the pitch and disrupting their steady, smooth passing game. Yaya was instrumental in that, and after 53 minutes he pounced on a mishit Michael Carrick pass, burst into the box and tucked his finish between goalkeeper Edwin van der Sar's legs, to score the winning goal.

City fans were in ecstasy. To many, the semi-final win meant more than the subsequent victory in the final. Not only had their team beaten their old rivals, they had deservedly done so, in a high-pressure match against a team which – when it came to derbies and to big matches – had a superiority complex. It was a sure sign that the "change in mentality" which Mancini had described as his biggest task when he took the job in east Manchester, was moving into its final phase. But this was purely a moment for the fans. For Mancini himself, it was a passage into the final, and there was still the more important matter of securing Champions League football: "I'm very happy for our supporters," he said. "They deserve to have a day like this afternoon, but we mustn't forget that we play another game. We only won the semi-final."

Another psychological barrier had been crossed with City's victory over the Reds. They had done it without Tevez, a player on whose goals the Blues had come to rely since his arrival in the summer of 2009. That was not lost on Mancini, who was aware of the Argentine star's ongoing restlessness and suspected that the Blues might have to plan for a future without him. "If we want to improve as a team and keep on winning then you have to play without important players like Carlos, Yaya Touré, or David Silva," he said. "It's important, but also important you improve as a team. Carlos is an important player for us and has scored more than 20 goals this year. Without him we are missing a fantastic striker who scores a lot of goals, but we have built a team this year. We have bought a lot of good players. When we are missing one or two important players we have a team, we always have a team."

After 31 years without a major Wembley cup final, the Blues now had one to contemplate at the end of the season, and to make it sweeter they had achieved it at the expense of their hated rivals. Mancini's problem was that he had to focus his players' minds on the league programme, and staving off Tottenham's attempt to dislodge them from fourth place. There were six league games left, four of them before the final on May 14, 2011.

Midfield enforcer Nigel de Jong had been a key man in Mancini's new, meaner City, helping them to the second best defensive record in the Premier League, and he gave the credit to the manager: "We've come this far, and that's down to him, the players and the staff as well – and we're still united as one. That's important if you want to be successful. In the defensive areas, he's really good. And you can see how good he is in the tactical points he makes too. We've not conceded many goals. The scoring rate could be better, but defensively, we've been good." That niggardly approach served City well as they went to Ewood Park nine days after the win over United and eked out a 1–0 win – and to make things better for Mancini, his much-criticized striker Dzeko, who had been angry and disillusioned at being left on the bench at Wembley, scored the winner.

The pressure was easing. Tottenham, who had been City's main rivals for that coveted fourth place, had gone on a run of just one win in nine games, perhaps paying the price for their Champions League exertions. That meant that City's 2–1 defeat by bogey team Everton – the Toffees' seventh win in eight league games between the two – hardly mattered. With three games left, City could make sure of fourth place by beating Spurs at Eastlands, just four days before they left for the FA Cup final.

In one sense, however, the defeat at Goodison Park had messed up Mancini's plans. Three points would have virtually secured fourth, and he could have rested key players against Spurs. Now there was sufficient doubt for him to need to play his front-line stars, ahead of a final against a tough, physical Stoke side. He had no need to worry. In a strange quirk of fate, big Spurs striker Crouch turned Milner's driven cross into his own net, at almost the very spot he had scored from to deny City a Champions League place almost a year earlier. On a night of jubilation at Eastlands, there was further cause for optimism in the return of Tevez as a late substitute, which meant he was in contention for a place in the cup final.

Mancini and his team had achieved his prime objective for the season but he was already eyeing third place, which would bring automatic qualification for the Champions League, and looking towards a bright new horizon. "In two or three years we could become one of the top teams in Europe. Now, it is important we try to get third. That is why it is so incredible that we lost three points against Everton after playing some fantastic football. We are two points behind Arsenal, and a lot of it is down to them. If they lose three points, we can do it – it is difficult but we will try. I sat down with the owners last summer and they told me they wanted Champions League football – now we have got it. We had some problems at the start of the season because players were coming back from the World Cup. Next year I think we will be better."

But the City fans were not yet thinking about possible encounters with Barcelona or Real Madrid in the hazy future of next season, or of getting third place. Such things could wait. They were contemplating their first FA Cup final since City had succumbed to the wizardry of Ricky Villa in losing to Spurs, back in 1981. They were pondering on Mancini's vow, within weeks of beginning his reign, to tear down the Stretford End banner.

Mancini again showed his faith in Balotelli by picking him to start, alongside Tevez. Again he was vindicated. City now looked a different team from the pragmatic, safety-conscious side which had begun the season, when Yaya Touré and David Silva were new and tentative. On the wide open spaces of Wembley, with the sun breaking through the clouds, they were simply too good for muscular Stoke, a side which had bullied them out of the FA Cup in 2009–10, inflicting Mancini's first defeat in the competition. He had since devised a tactic to nullify Stoke's strengths, getting his players to press Stoke high up the pitch to try to prevent the long balls on which they thrive, and telling his players to concentrate on not giving away throw-ins in the final third, or corners or free kicks.

The difference in class between the teams was obvious in the first half as Yaya Touré, Tevez, Silva and Balotelli carved through the Potters at will. It just needed a goal, and until it arrived, the sky blue half of the stadium remained convinced that, even after having dispatched United's aristocrats to get there, Typical City would blow it against the journeymen of Stoke.

In fact the moment they dreaded seemed to have arrived just minutes into the second half when Stoke's leggy striker Kenwyne Jones managed to escape Lescott and bear down on goal. His problem was that Hart had, all season, justified Mancini's decision to prefer him to Given. He would end the season with the Premier League Golden Gloves award for the keeper with the most clean sheets, after achieving a club record 18 shut-outs. When Jones tried to slip the ball past him, Hart made a vital save, one which would be every bit as important as Yaya Touré's winning goal.

City had been in control, with Yaya smashing a shot narrowly wide and Balotelli forcing keeper Thomas Sorensen into a spectacular save. But as the game wore on, Stoke began to sense an upset, and Mancini had to act. He took off Gareth Barry, who had been an injury doubt going into the game, and introduced width in the shape of Adam Johnson, while moving Silva to a more central position. The switch worked almost instantly as Balotelli's backheel sent Silva haring for the byline. He pulled the ball back for the Italian striker, and when his shot was blocked, Yaya arrived to gleefully smash a shot left-footed through the crowd and into the net. Now all that was required was nerve and organization to close out the game – something City had not always been good at during the league season.

But this new Blue team were not about to be denied, and it was Tevez who lifted the trophy to bring an end to 35 barren years amid the tears and cheers of the fans. Mancini had thrown his arms wide and looked to the heavens, but his joy at winning trophies is always fleeting. Within an hour of the moment of triumph, he is already restlessly looking to the next challenge.

He didn't have far to look for the next challenge this time, as the Blues would face Stoke again at Eastlands three days later. With third-placed Arsenal stumbling towards the finish line, having lost two out of three, Mancini felt that another victory over Stoke and triumph at Bolton on the final day might just secure automatic qualification for the Champions League, cutting out two unnecessary and potentially tricky qualifying games in August.

Mancini instantly banned his players from celebrating the cup triumph with a boozy celebration, and warned the supporters they should get used to the sight of their team hoisting trophies: "We won the FA Cup. It is an important trophy, but we need to improve more to take another step and win the title. It was important to start to win because when you start to win, afterwards everything will be easier. We want to try to match United. We have got to the Champions League, that was our first target, and we won the FA Cup. It is very important for this club."

The Gunners gave City another boost the day after the cup final, by losing at home to Aston Villa. Suddenly third place was now in City's own grasp. They were in no mood to be denied, and when a demoralized Stoke rolled up in Manchester they were taken apart as two world-class Tevez goals, either side of a Lescott header, saw them leapfrog Arsenal. Now they just needed to match Arsène Wenger's side's result on the final day of the season, and they would secure their highest finish since Brian Kidd's goals helped to fire them to second place behind Liverpool in 1977.

Lescott and Dzeko grabbed the goals in a 2–0 win at Bolton, Arsenal drew, and after scrambling for half of the season to hold on to fourth, the Blues had secured third place by a clear three points. Champions League football was a certainty, which meant that planning for the following season could move onto a higher footing.

Mancini immediately went on the offensive, urging the club to buy four or five players who would allow him to compete on four trophy fronts. The club's executives, all too aware that Uefa's new "financial fair play" rules would begin to take effect the following season, were playing down the number and magnitude of the signings. But Mancini was sending out his own message, and talking directly to chairman Khaldoon al Mubarak. He also appeared to set his own deadline for the deals to be done, saying he wanted the new players in within 40 days, so they could join pre-season and be perfectly prepared for the new campaign.

The manager was full of praise for the chairman: "Khaldoon is a clever man and a really good man. He understands what the squad needs for next year. He understands that we need to improve, because in one year it is impossible that we can improve 200 per cent, that we can play Barcelona and beat them easily. We need to work and we need to bring in other players. When you play in the Champions League, you should play with 11 good players. Playing in the Premier League three days later is really, really difficult if you don't have a good squad, if you don't have 23, 24 good players. If you don't have that, you could have what has happened to Tottenham this season. They put all their energy into the Champions League, and then they lost a lot of points in the Premier League.

"There are many players that want to play for City. We have time – 40 days to buy players who can help us to improve. We are not close but we are not too far from some of them, but all the clubs want the good players. This year we can work in pre-season with our players – last year we didn't. This is important – to work for a month with the players is vital for the team. That is how you build a team. And we will have other players who have just played in the Champions League."

All that was left was for the team to show off the trophy, as Manchester staged its first Blue victory parade for many years. After an open-top bus parade from the Town Hall to the stadium, Mancini and his players were greeted by the supporters. The manager handed the credit to his players, praised owner Sheikh Mansour, and dedicated the triumph to the fans. It was a night of celebration, adulation, and high optimism for the following season.

Over at Old Trafford, the mocking "35 Years" banner which Mancini had vowed to tear down had been quietly removed from the Stretford End. United fans briefly discussed replacing it with one which read "43 Years", to denote the length of time since their neighbours had lifted the league trophy. Someone pointed out that, with the Blues clearly on the march, and sure to strengthen in the summer, that banner might have an embarrassingly short life, and the idea was dropped.

Chapter Nine
Mario, Carlos and Roberto

One was said to be "unmanageable", a one-man media feeding frenzy. The other appeared to be incorrigible, a player who "plays when he wants" according to jeering opposition fans. And yet with the twin storms of Mario Balotelli and Carlos Tevez raging around him and neighbours United in hot pursuit, Roberto Mancini honed a title-winning team. The harbingers of doom, some of them wearing replica sky-blue shirts, had been convinced it would all end messily, and that either the ongoing saga of Tevez or the unpredictability of Balotelli, or perhaps the two together, would be the club's downfall.

Former City star Rodney Marsh predicted on a national radio show that if City lost the title, having been five points clear at one stage, Mancini's handling of the Tevez affair would earn him the sack. The fact that the manager eventually knitted his two wayward stars back into the mesh of his first-team squad, and that both played their part in finally bringing the Premier League title to the Etihad Stadium – as the City of Manchester Stadium was renamed during the summer of 2011 – was a triumph on a personal level for the City boss.

The management of Tevez was the first and biggest challenge of Roberto Mancini's career at Manchester City, while his handling of Balotelli, ranging from a paternal arm around the shoulders to the launching of luggage across a dressing-room, might still determine whether he turns out to be world superstar or wastrel. Critics outside the club were aghast that Mancini could allow Balotelli's behaviour – sometimes simply wacky, sometimes damaging to his team's fortunes – to slide by, punished by a fine, a harsh word, or a place on the bench. The prevailing view was that José Mourinho, who had inherited the teenage prodigy from Mancini at Inter and had dismissed him as "simply unmanageable", had got it spot on. And those who had labelled Tevez as a "mercenary" also felt vindicated as his career at City started to come apart at the seams, fuelled by homesickness and rows between his adviser and the City hierarchy, and fiery exchanges between the player and Mancini.

Mancini's patience with Balotelli, and his willingness to forgive Tevez, were rooted in his own past. He remembered only too well the impetuosity of his youth, and has regretted the stubborn refusal to apologize which cost him two and a half years of his international career.

When Mancini walked into his office at Carrington for the first time in late December 2009, it was apparent that Tevez would be a key figure in the shaping of his early days at the club. The Argentine had started to live up to his world-class billing, and his six strikes in Mancini's first three games in charge made it plain that there was a high degree of reliance on the club's top wage-earner. Mancini recognized his own drive and fire in the squat little Argentine, and was prepared to cut the player slack when he needed it. As the Blues prepared for an FA Cup fifth-round tie against Stoke in February, news came through that Tevez's estranged, pregnant wife Vanesa had been taken to hospital in Buenos Aires. She had returned to her native country, unhappy and unable to settle in Manchester, and in the midst of marital difficulties. Tevez was granted compassionate leave to fly back to Argentina as Vanesa gave birth to their second daughter, Katie, ten weeks early, and the child was placed in a special care unit. Mancini gave Tevez permission to remain in Argentina as long as the child was in intensive care, but the City attack was toothless without him. With a trip to play leaders Chelsea looming and the new baby out of danger, Mancini told Tevez he expected the player back in time to play – he flew in to Heathrow, met the squad at their team hotel the day before the game and promptly scored twice in a shock 4–2 victory.

In a newspaper interview just weeks later, Tevez grumbled that Mancini had not improved him as a player, and about the manager's double training sessions. Mancini was mystified and unhappy at Tevez's words, and called the player in for a chat, during which he reminded him that he had only staged four double training sessions since he started five months earlier, and that Tevez had only been involved in one. Mancini's message to the grumbling player was stark and to the point, and he made no secret of it: "It's the same for Tevez as for all players. If they don't want to stay here, it is best they go to another team. When a player works in a team, he must be happy to work in that team, or it is no good for the club, the squad or the player. My opinion is that a player has to be happy to work with a team, and if he is not it is better to change squad."

The disagreement was forgotten, and Tevez picked up two of the club's player of the year awards for his 29 goals and all-round contribution. The club made it plain he was "not for sale, at any price". That summer, Tevez expressed his disillusionment with football and talked of retiring, but he was perked up by a City spending spree, and Mancini tried to tap into Tevez's inner energy and fire by making him captain, taking the armband off Kolo Touré. The idea was to try to bring Tevez closer to the squad, and inspire him, in the way that Diego Maradona, one of Mancini's old Serie A opponents, had lifted his game at Napoli after being made skipper. It seemed to work, as Tevez began the season in good form and showed signs of forming an understanding with new signing David Silva.

There was always a moan bubbling beneath the surface with the Argentine, but that has never been a concern for Mancini, who was also a grumbler as a player. For him it is a positive sign: he sees it as showing a desire to win, and seeking perfection from one's self and from team-mates, and even from the manager. The two men clashed again at half time of a home game against Newcastle, and had to be separated. But they shook hands at the end of the game and met to discuss the incident the following day; and at that meeting the player asked for, and was given, an extra day off to visit his family after a forthcoming international match. Mancini was mystified by the fuss surrounding his dressing-room row with Tevez: "What happened, happens in our dressing-room," he said. "And when it matters it is good that it happens. Against Newcastle, City slept in the first half, and the confrontation with Tevez was the alarm call everybody needed. We sorted everything before the restart. When I took him off at the end we shook hands."

Trips back to Buenos Aires, however, simply seemed to make Tevez's homesickness worse. He was living in a Cheshire mansion, a long way from his family, and was finding it tough, something that not even City's top salary of around £230,000 a week could cure. When the player suffered a thigh injury at the end of October, he again asked for permission to return to Argentina, for treatment and to visit his daughters, and was allowed to go.

The two men continued to have rows, but both saw nothing wrong in that. Tevez later said of Mancini: "The things that we do behind the scenes at the club, both he and I, are always for the good of City … anything that goes on between us on the pitch or in the dressing-room stays there, and he and I keep on fighting for the club … Roberto and I get on and I back him 100 per cent. We discuss lots of things both in public and in private. We are both passionate football people and we both want the same things for Manchester City, and that is success."

It was hard to determine Tevez's state of mind. In December 2010, days after appearing on City's website talking of how happy he was at the club, the player asked permission for a three-day break, as he would miss the meeting with his old club West Ham owing to a suspension. Sympathetic to his difficulties in being away from his family, the club acceded, and even allowed him to extend the break by a day when he asked for it. They were expecting Tevez to fly to Buenos Aires – instead, he headed for a sunshine break in Tenerife with a girlfriend.

To make matters worse, while he was there, he submitted a transfer request, saying that his relationship with "club executives" was beyond repair. He said he had "no personal issue with the manager" and that he had told the club he wanted to leave in the summer, as he wanted to be closer to his family. City felt that money, and his adviser Kia Joorabchian, were behind the unrest. Accusations flew, and the manager was left picking up the pieces and trying to keep his side on track for their double aim of finishing in the top four and winning a trophy.

Mancini's response was to make it plain that he would not be allowing Tevez to leave in the January transfer window, saying:

"We started the season, which is an important season for us, with this group of players, and we have this group for this year. Carlos is an important player for us, so I told him he must stay here." The manager also made light of Tevez's declaration of unhappiness: "I hope he can continue to be unhappy because he has scored ten goals, has played very well, and we are in this position in the table! I hope he can be this unhappy for the rest of the season!"

Mancini and chairman Khaldoon al Mubarak both spoke to the player, and he withdrew his request a week later, as the team prepared for the home game with Everton – which could have sent the Blues top for Christmas, had they not lost it. The crisis had been temporarily averted, and Tevez was given a new strike partner in the January transfer window as Dzeko joined from Wolfsburg. It was not long before the Argentine was back in the goalscoring groove, but seeds of doubt had been sown in Mancini's mind. He knew he could have built a title-winning team around Tevez as the fulcrum of the attack, but he could not count on a man who had repeatedly talked of wanting to leave. The manager needed someone he could rely on, and long before the end of the 2010–11 season he was identifying the man he needed – Tevez's Argentina team-mate Sergio Aguero.

The positive for Mancini was that no matter how much complaining the player did off the field, no matter how many times he and his advisers made worrying noises about the future, the manager could be sure of one thing. The moment Tevez crossed the white line, you always got 100 per cent effort from him, and his contribution to an excellent City season could not be denied. He again top-scored that season, with 23 goals, more than the next two players in the list – Balotelli and Yaya Touré – put together.

After speaking to Tevez at the end of a successful season, Mancini said: "He is a fantastic player, a fantastic striker and I think he will stay here next year." Within 24 hours, however, Joorabchian was suggesting the opposite, and saying Tevez had given Mancini no assurances at all. Mancini had heard enough, and with the FA Cup and Champions League qualification in the bag and his position strengthened, Mancini flew to Abu Dhabi to meet with Khaldoon al Mubarak and Sheikh Mansour and tell them what he needed for the following season. Top of the list was Atletico Madrid's dashing young striker Aguero, who had many of Tevez's attributes and none of the attitude.

Tevez's next words on the matter came during a popular Argentine television chat show, when he seemed intent on wiping out the few remaining shreds of goodwill he retained among the Manchester public, Red or Blue. Asked about life in the city, he said: "There's nothing to do in Manchester. There are two restaurants and everything's small. It rains all the time, you can't go anywhere. There comes a moment where you say 'Where am I going to go with my family?' and you begin to feel bad … Once I leave, I will not return to Manchester, not for a holiday, not anything."

Early in July, while on duty with Argentina as they hosted the Copa America, he made his unhappiness official, informing the club he wanted to leave, and citing the heartache of being separated from his family. City were happy for him to leave, as he was increasingly an embarrassment, but they made it plain that they would not be bullied into allowing him to leave on the cheap – he would go on their terms, or not at all, and the price tag they slapped on him was £50 million. The Blues were actually prepared to release him if a bid of around £38 million came in, as that was the price they were close to agreeing with Atletico for Aguero.

The only realistic bid came from Brazilian club Corinthians, but they failed to provide assurances that they had the money. City bought the "replacement" Aguero anyway, for £38 million, and at the start of the 2011–12 season, Mancini had four A-grade strikers in his squad – Tevez, Aguero, Dzeko and Balotelli. Each had a question mark hanging over his head. Could Balotelli straighten out his act? Could Dzeko improve his goalscoring ratio? Could Aguero adapt to life in the physically more demanding Premier League? And would Tevez knuckle back down to life in wet, cheerless, restaurant-free Manchester?

Aguero and Dzeko began the season with a remarkable burst of 14 goals between them in the first five league games, with Tevez and Balotelli watching from the bench. Unhappy at going from hero to sub, Tevez also learned that he had been given a pay cut – his transfer request had nullified a loyalty bonus, costing him a possible £6 million. As the team headed for a prestige Champions League game at Bayern Munich, he had another reason to be in a grumpy mood, having been fined and given three points on his licence for speeding in his Bentley Continental GT. A grumpy player left on the bench, and a manager who saw his side defend badly to go 2–0 down by half time, was a volatile combination.

In the second half, Mancini gave the word via fitness conditioner Ivan Carminati for Tevez to warm up, which he did, but as he returned to the bench, Mancini took off Dzeko and replaced him with defensive midfielder Nigel de Jong. It was a tactic often used by Mancini, making a defensive switch first and then minutes later making a more offensive one. But it brought a furious reaction from

Dzeko, who had been desperate to impress in his first match back in Germany since his move from Wolfsburg.

Tevez would later relate his version of the incident: "I was kind of in a bad mood and when Mancini decided to replace Edin Dzeko with Nigel de Jong when we were losing 2–0, I thought it was a defensive substitution and started to sit back on the bench. I had already warmed up for ten minutes, and he had this attitude that he wants to lose 2–0 instead of 4–0. So I sat down and at the same time Dzeko came off, really angry, and had a go at Mancini. He sat down next to him and they started to have an argument. Dzeko was speaking Bosnian and Mancini would swear at him in Italian – it was a real mess.

"So I went to sit down and he didn't see me because he was having this discussion. But then he turned around and saw me, and you can imagine what happened. He's in the middle of an argument, told me to keep on warming up, and treated me like a dog. When he spoke to me in that tone of voice I said, 'No, I'm not going out.' I was willing to play, but the coach was in such a foul mood because he had that argument with Dzeko, he started on me as well, and started swearing at me. That was him, because I was very calm, just sitting on the bench. You can see from the footage that I was calm, just talking with Pablo Zabaleta, and Mancini was saying some horrible things to me."

Mancini took Tevez's unwillingness as a refusal to go onto the pitch, and was incandescent. Pitch-side TV reporters could not help but notice the row, with Mancini shouting and gesticulating, and Tevez muttering to Pablo Zabaleta and Aleks Kolarov on the bench.

Asked about the incident afterwards, Mancini said: "I am really disappointed with Carlos for this, really disappointed. If he was another player, maybe. This can't happen at a top club, that one player refuses to go and help his team-mates in an important match like tonight. I decided to change Edin with Nigel because I wanted to keep the score down and not to concede a third goal. After five minutes Carlos was ready to go in. Afterwards he refused to warm up again. He refused to go on the pitch.

"If one player earns a lot of money and plays for Man City in the Champions League, and he behaves like this, for me he can't play. Never. I think he was disappointed because he didn't go first change – maybe. But when I said Carlos – go, with 35 minutes to the end, I think that in 35 minutes we can change the result. What I said to Carlos is between me, him and the team. If we want to improve like a team, like a squad, Carlos cannot play with us. With me, no. It is finished."

As Tevez emerged from the dressing-room after the game, he was grabbed by a Sky TV interviewer, and Pedro Marques – a Portuguese member of City's video analysis crew – was corralled in to interpret, with the player keen to give his account: As translated by Marquez, the player's words to Sky were: "I didn't feel right to play, so I told him I couldn't play. I have always done my best for the club and was top scorer last year. If he doesn't want to play me again that's up to him."

The following day that version was quickly dismissed as a poor translation, and Tevez put out a statement apologizing to City fans for the incident but claiming: "I had warmed up and was ready to play. This is not the right time to get into specific details as to why this did not happen. But I wish to state that I never refused to play. There was some confusion on the bench and I believe my position may have been misunderstood. Going forward I am ready to play when required and to fulfil my obligations." A refusal to play would have been a gross breach of contract, and Tevez could have been sacked and possibly pursued through the court for the cost of his own transfer value. City acted quickly, suspending the player for an initial two weeks as they began a full club review of the incident, and allowed him to return to Argentina once he had been interviewed.

After that review, City informed the player he would face a disciplinary process for breaches of contract, but Mancini made one last effort to offer the player an olive branch. Tevez flew back into London the night before his club suspension expired, as he was due back in training. Having boarded a train to Manchester, Tevez received a phone call from Mancini inviting him to meet at the manager's house in Alderley Edge. In the early hours of the morning, Mancini offered him the chance to apologize, both to him and to Khaldoon al Mubarak, which would have seen him back in the squad. Tevez refused to say sorry, instead insisting that Mancini should be the one offering apologies.

He was ordered to report to the Carrington training centre an hour after the rest of the squad the following day, and he was sent for a 60-minute fitness assessment away from team-mates. For almost two weeks, Tevez had to train on his own, or with the young professionals of the elite development squad. He became Carrington's forgotten man as City continued their storming start to the season, hammering United 6–1 at Old Trafford along the way. But Mancini's version of events in Munich had not been supported by the evidence gathered by the club investigation, and instead of being accused of refusing to play, Tevez faced a lesser charge of refusing to warm up. Essentially it had been a communication failure.

Three days after City's crushing derby win, Tevez was fined four weeks' wages, around £800,000, after being found guilty of

five breaches of his contract. That fine would be halved when the
Professional Footballers' Association, who have to be consulted if
a club wants to fine one of their members more than two weeks'
wages, said it felt the punishment was too harsh. Mancini had no
more time for the matter, referring to it only by saying that his focus
was on fighting United for the title and that "other situations are
not important". Tevez, still refusing to say sorry, continued to train
apart from the first-team squad, and finally accepted the fine at the
beginning of November.

When the squad broke up for international duty after a 3–2 win
at Queen's Park Rangers on November 5, the elite development
squad, with whom Tevez had been training, was given a week off.
Tevez's advisers asked the club's acting chief executive John Macbeath
if he could also take time off, but under Mancini's instructions the
request was refused, the manager saying the errant player needed to
do extra fitness work after his enforced lay-off. Another request, to
Mancini's assistant Fausto Salsano, was also turned down, although
Tevez's people said Salsano's answer was ambiguous. A spokesman for
the player said repeated phone calls to Mancini had been ignored.

Tevez took his chances and left anyway, boarding a flight for
Paris on Monday, November 7, to catch a connection to Buenos
Aires. When he failed to show up at Carrington on Wednesday
morning, he was again in breach of contract, and City demanded
an explanation, which was not forthcoming. Mancini had himself
taken a break to visit his family in Italy, and on his return he faced
more questions about Tevez. The media hungered for any snippet
about the player who had gone absent without leave, while the fans
– enjoying the best start to a season in their history – were simply fed
up with it. Mancini was weary of answering questions about it. It was

all the same to him whether Tevez was in Buenos Aires or jogging around a training pitch with the young players. He was unavailable for selection, and that put him out of the manager's mind.

Mancini's patience with the English media had been exemplary, but he showed signs of getting snappy at the repeated questions about the absentee Tevez while his team were storming away at the top of the league and playing brilliant football. Tevez, meanwhile, was playing golf and partying back home in Argentina, while Milan plotted to buy him on the cheap in January. City fans were furious, and wanted to know whether the player was still picking up his huge salary while living the good life in his homeland. City consistently refused to give any details, and with good reason. They had instigated another internal disciplinary process, and it was important not to leak any details, as that could compromise any action against Tevez.

By the end of January 2012, they were ready to reveal the truth. Tevez's troubles with the club, dating back to his transfer request a year earlier, had cost him around £9.3 million in lost salary and bonuses, and club fines. They had stopped his wages as soon as possible after he failed to report for training, and charged him with gross misconduct, resulting in a fine of £1.2 million, a record club fine in football. Tevez's camp said that the player had agreed to waive his wages, in his absence. City also slapped down Milan's continual public pronouncements about buying the player, telling them to put up or shut up. The transfer deadline passed, and Tevez was left with a stark choice – either return to City or stay away, losing more salary and possibly facing further sanctions, including possible sacking and legal action to recover his £38 million worth.

Joorabchian said that Tevez's problem had been his "feuds" with the manager: "You think about last Christmas when Carlos wanted to leave and it was all to do with feuds with the manager, and I think that just carried on and on. There was a point when Carlos did say, 'I can't get on here.' And he is not the only one. You have to reflect back. Bellamy had to leave Manchester City in an awkward way, Adebayor has had to leave Manchester City in an awkward way, Shay Given has had to leave Manchester City in a semi-awkward way, Wayne Bridge has been isolated and is not even training with the first team. He is not alone, Carlos."

Mancini said there was no problem between him and Tevez, and responded by naming the player in his 25-man Premier League squad for the remainder of the season, after talks between Joorabchian and Macbeath paved the way for a reconciliation. The manager said that it was "possible" the player could play again that season, but his position remained unchanged from the days following their clash in Munich – the player had to say he was sorry first. There were further signs of a thaw in the relationship when Tevez dropped his appeal to the Premier League over his £1.2 million fine, indicating an acceptance of his punishment for leaving the club without permission.

Tevez prepared to fly back to England, but had one last dig at the manager. Speaking about the Munich incident in a TV interview in Buenos Aires, he said Mancini had "treated me like a dog". He was also less than complimentary about the way the City boss had handled things: "I think that's where Mancini got things wrong. If we had a problem, we could have sorted it out in a different way. Mancini is a winner. And I'm a winner too. None of us like to lose. If it's true that Mancini said he will welcome me back if I'm fit, then I like those quotes, but he also said I was never going to be playing for him again. So I don't know. I'll do my best to be available and play.

Mancini's position got stronger when Kun Aguero arrived. I don't know if he would have done the things he did if this was last season. But he never said anything. He got a better team this season and felt like making the decision."

Tevez flew back on Valentine's Day, but it did not appear that he and Mancini were about to kiss and make up. The manager responded to the "dog" accusations by suggesting the problem was quite the opposite, and that he had made a problem for himself by indulging the player: "I totally disagree with Carlos and what he says because I have never treated him badly. Maybe it's the opposite. I have treated him too well, always."

Within a week, Tevez had back-tracked, and issued a statement in which he "sincerely and unreservedly" apologized. The coast was clear for his comeback – all he needed now was to get fit, and for the pragmatic Mancini, it felt as if he had a new signing, just as the season was reaching a thrilling climax.

***

Balotelli presented Mancini with a wholly different challenge. The young Italian was a precocious and prodigiously gifted striker, but one who appeared to be scarred by a difficult early life, when he was given up by his Ghanaian family and adopted by white Italians. He had suffered the barbs of racism as a kid, and was pricked by them again as his football career took off, frequently being singled out by the extremist morons who inhabit some Italian football stadiums.

He is a complex individual, intelligent and thoughtful despite being dismissed as a buffoon by those who have not met him. "He takes some getting used to" was the early verdict of one of the senior City professionals, although it was said with a grin rather than a grimace. "Like your annoying little brother, a real pain, but you can't help but love him – most of the time" was the opinion of another member of the City staff.

When Mancini first encountered him he remembered his own teenage years, his impatience to achieve great things, his realization that coaches and referees are often wrong, and his penchant for saying and doing the wrong thing. He also recognized a supreme talent in Balotelli, not hesitating to introduce him to the Inter first team at a crucial phase of a title-winning season, just as their lead at the top appeared to be crumbling around his ears.

Mourinho had shown no such patience, believing the young player was impenetrable, beyond help. Mancini does not think so, even though the lad has driven him to distraction at times. There are three Balotellis: the public perception of an eccentric, scowling, half-crazy kid, fuelled by wild stories about his escapades, some of them true, most of them nonsense; the real person, a complex, shy, sensitive boy who seems to crave the spotlight, but loathes the consequences of being in it; and the one Mancini concerns himself with – an extraordinarily talented footballer.

Like Tevez, Balotelli is often indulged by Mancini. The manager advises him about his occasional smoking habit, but doesn't lecture. He played Balotelli in the 6–1 derby win despite a recent incident with fireworks in which the player's house was almost burnt down. And he didn't fine the player for breaking a club curfew ahead of a game. But once he is on the training pitch, or out on the field for real, the indulgence ends. When Balotelli tried an unnecessary spinning back-heel in a friendly game against Los Angeles Galaxy,

Mancini was furious and substituted him immediately, even though the game did not matter. That incident, and the fact that Mancini felt he was not working hard enough in training, saw him start the 2011–12 season on the bench.

When Balotelli joined the club in the summer of 2010, he quickly showed the assembled press his trademark frown, baulking at the suggestion he had a "bad boy" reputation in Italy. "I am a normal guy," he said. Mancini, no doubt remembering his own salad days, weighed in with: "All of us are said to be bad boys when we are young. But I have worked with Mario before and he is a normal person. He is a young player, only 20 years old, who can do a lot in the Premier League. He has all the qualities needed to become a fantastic player."

Balotelli had a typically headline-grabbing start to his City career. On his debut at Timisoara, he scored the winner after going on as a substitute, argued with the referee and an opponent, and sustained a knee injury which would require surgery. The following week in Manchester, confused by driving on the left in a left-hand-drive car, he had an accident and wrote off his Audi R8. When police attending the accident asked why he had £5,000 in his car, the answer came, "Because I am rich."

The off-field stuff was of no great concern to Mancini, unless it impacted on his football. The problem with Balotelli was that unlike Tevez, you could never be sure what you would get on the pitch. After returning from his knee injury, Balotelli clearly found the physical nature of English football difficult. At West Brom he showed his talent with two match-winning goals, and was then red-carded for flicking a boot at Youssouf Mulumbu. City's appeal against the decision and the three-match suspension was rejected. Defending his player, Mancini drew comparisons with his younger self and denied that Balotelli was given special treatment: "It is about getting the best out of him, and you have to remember he is still young. I can see a bit of myself in him at that age. I used to shout sometimes and get angry. When you are 20, it is impossible to behave well all the time. We are dealing with different personalities and characters, so of course I have a different approach, depending on the player. But there is no favouritism, and he is not crazy, as some people have suggested. He's just the same as other 20-year-olds."

As Balotelli prepared to come back from the suspension, Mancini spoke of his reasons for cutting him some slack: "I know how good Mario can become. He could develop into one of the top players in the world within two years, because he has everything. He is young and needs time, but if he wants, he can become a top player. There are a few players in the past like him. Cantona, Ronaldo, Rooney. That is the level he can reach. I think if Mario uses his head and thinks clearly, he can do that. He just needs to change his character a bit. Not completely, but just enough. People will try to wind him up, but he needs to understand that he must show different behaviour on the pitch, because if he plays every game, I think he will make a difference."

Mancini was also unmoved as the newspaper headlines again screamed about City's supposed dressing-room disharmony after a painful tackle by Jerome Boateng in training had led to a tussle with the Italian. The giant woolly "chicken hat", his tangled love life, his confetti of parking tickets, and a thousand and one stories were meat and drink to the English media, but Mancini could not care less. He was more concerned about the player's refusal to celebrate goals. Balotelli's view was that he was paid to score goals, so had no reason to celebrate something which was his duty. Mancini feels that fun is as vital an ingredient as fury in a footballer, saying: "You need to smile to play football. That is the best thing you can do." The manager has admitted several times that he speaks to Balotelli most days, trying to drum into him what it takes to be a truly world-class player, and once said that his antics sometimes make him want to "punch him in the head". Balotelli's answer was typically impish: "He can't – I do Thai boxing!"

But in the winter of 2010–11, Balotelli was under-performing, missing family and friends in Italy, and his reputation was earning him unwarranted yellow cards. He was still showing glimpses of his raw talent, not least with a hat-trick in a 4–0 hammering of Aston Villa, but Mancini was not happy with his player, feeling he was not progressing as he should and was not listening to his advice.

Things came to a head during the Europa League tie against Dynamo Kiev. The first leg, in ice-bound Ukraine, was bizarre, as Balotelli walked out for the second half – after a listless first half – clutching a swelling beneath his eye. He was quickly substituted, the explanation being that he was allergic to the type of grass Dynamo used on their pitch, and City lost 2–0. In the second leg, Balotelli's mounting frustration resulted in him leaping and raking his studs down the chest of defender Goran Popov for a straight red card. The ten-man Blues managed a 1–0 win on the night but went out. Mancini finally snapped, calling the young player an "idiot", saying he wished he had not signed him, and hurling his bag at him across the dressing-room.

Balotelli then heard that he had been dropped by Italy, and the following week he landed in more hot water when he threw a dart at a youth team player at the club's Carrington training base. Mancini handed the baton over to his player, saying: "Now the time has come for him to help himself, and to understand the mistakes he is making. Otherwise he risks throwing away his abilities, which are immense. He has scored some tremendous goals this season. If he does not, then everybody in England will begin to make him a target – starting off with the referees. He knows this could be a fantastic experience for him here in England. He can be one of the best players in Europe. Everything Mario does becomes big news. If he goes into a restaurant and speaks with a woman, it is said that maybe five women speak with him. It's news."

The moment of truth for Balotelli arrived in April 2011. Tevez had damaged a hamstring five days before the FA Cup semi-final against Manchester United, and Mancini took a deep breath before selecting his enigmatic young star, urging him to become "a hero". He need not have worried, as Balotelli rose to the occasion, leading the line superbly and being named man of the match as the Blues beat the old enemy 1–0 and booked a cup final spot. Even a spot of bother at the end of the game, when Balotelli showed his City shirt to dejected United fans, winking at a furious Reds skipper Rio Ferdinand as he protested, could not quell the idea that he had taken a step forward. In fact this all helped to make the player more popular with the City fans, who were starting to sing songs about Balotelli's feats and eccentricities.

Balotelli cited Mancini's fury after the red card against Kiev as a turning point for him: "Mancini was angry, but I prefer someone to be direct. I hate people who say to my face 'Mario, you are good' and then tell other people behind my back 'Mario is s***.' Roberto says what he has to say – he never lies and that is what I like about him. Mancini is doing what Mourinho couldn't do. Mourinho couldn't understand me. They are both great managers, but they are different men. Mancini supports me, Mourinho was different. Whenever I had a problem, Mourinho always went against me. Maybe it is because we have the same character. Mancini savaged me after the Kiev game, but that was in private. In public, he has always supported me."

The player could not stay out of the news, even in the summer break. He was fined for doing 80kph in a 30kph zone while home in Italy, and it was revealed he would be called to give evidence at an inquiry into organized crime in Naples after being given a guided tour of the city's notorious mob areas. Then he returned to training wearing a T-shirt emblazoned with guns and a knife, drawing criticism from anti-gun campaigners. Mancini was unmoved by all of those peripheral things, but the player's showboating at Los Angeles Galaxy again caused him to come down hard.

Balotelli was sidelined as Aguero and Dzeko began the 2011–12 season in fine style, and when he did get his chance, his performances were patchy. There were still glimpses of his supreme talent – a goal to break spirited Everton, a nonchalant finish to begin a 4–0 rout of Blackburn, and an overhead kick against Aston Villa. But he again saved his best for United, scoring a brilliantly precise opening goal, adding a second and teasing Jonny Evans into a red card offence as the Blues ran riot at Old Trafford. That first goal saw Balotelli lift his shirt above his head to reveal a T-shirt asking "Why Always Me?" – an iconic moment. Two nights earlier, Cheshire Fire Brigade had been called to Balotelli's £3 million home after friends of the player, messing with fireworks, had set fire to a bathroom, causing damage costing £400,000.

Balotelli was a heady cocktail. On the pitch, he was scoring important goals and sometimes going missing. Off it, he was in danger of passing into urban legend as stories popped up about him at every turn – he had dressed as Santa Claus and handed out money to Manchester's homeless; he had called in at a pub and bought everyone a drink; he had dropped £1,000 in a church collection plate. All untrue, but his life was quickly becoming a tangle of fact and fiction.

Mancini's concern was that the hoo-ha and the "wild child" image were landing him in unwarranted trouble with referees, an impression that was reinforced when an innocuous, apparently accidental elbow to Liverpool defender Martin Skrtel got him a red card at Anfield. Just when life appeared to be returning to normal – or as normal as it gets for Balotelli – he landed in more hot water after tangling with Tottenham's Scott Parker in an important January match at the Etihad Stadium. At the time it looked as if the City striker simply stumbled into Parker, who then lay on the ground clutching his head. Referee Howard Webb allowed play to continue, and Balotelli ended up scoring the winner from a last-minute penalty. However, slow-motion replays appeared to show Balotelli stamping on the prone Parker, and after Webb said he had not seen the incident at the time, Balotelli was hit with a four-match retrospective ban.

City fans raged that the Blues were being picked on and that Sky Sports were setting the FA's disciplinary agenda. Skipper Vincent Kompany was already serving a four-match ban for a red card in the FA Cup defeat by Manchester United, and other players were getting away with offences which seemed more serious but had not been given the same television scrutiny. Mancini's response was much calmer than what he might have said in his youth: "I think playing a lot of games is also difficult for referees. The refs sometimes are tired

– to play every two or three days is difficult for the players, and for the referee."

The next problem came when Balotelli was spotted in a Liverpool strip club, breaking a club curfew ahead of the game against Bolton. Mancini fined him a week's wages, about £125,000, but still picked him for the game – and he scored in a 2–0 victory. Balotelli promised to repay his manager's faith by helping him win the Premier League, but he had a funny way of trying to fulfil that promise. Hauled off at half time against Chelsea after missing a great chance, two weeks later he got involved in an argument with Aleks Kolarov about who should take a free kick as City trailed 3–1 at home to Sunderland. He was booed by some City fans for that, although his stunning late goal as the Blues hit back to draw 3–3 meant partial redemption.

With the title on the line, and City flagging as United put on a spurt, Balotelli hit his lowest point at Arsenal on Easter Sunday. He should have been sent off for a terrible early challenge on midfielder Alex Song, but he did not learn his lesson and a second yellow late in the game heaped more misery on Mancini as City lost 1–0 and went eight points behind in the title race. Mancini appeared to suggest that he would "probably" sell Balotelli in the summer, expecting the FA to bring his season to a close with a hefty ban. The manager later claimed he had misunderstood the question.

However, Balotelli still had at least one last, hugely important part to play in the Blues' destiny ... and so did Tevez.

Chapter Ten
Noisier Neighbours

Roberto Mancini and Sir Alex Ferguson sat in the Manchester United manager's office, sharing a glass of red, and talking about the merits of Italian wine. They might have been spending a lazy summer afternoon in a Genoa quayside café. But there was an elephant in the room, a topic of conversation that had to be avoided at all costs. Mancini's City had just beaten Ferguson's United in the Manchester derby – only their second win at Old Trafford in 38 years – in fact they had destroyed, humiliated and outclassed them, by six goals to one. Ferguson would later call it the worst day of his football life.

In one brilliant, barmy afternoon, the Blues had swept away all doubts that they had what it takes to win the Premier League title. The victory signalled not just a seismic shift in the balance of power in Manchester football, but a sign that English football might never be the same again. Disbelieving, demoralized United fans left the stadium in droves, as the 3,000 away fans danced and laughed, and jeered as never before.

Mancini clearly enjoyed the moment, but by the time he reached the City dressing-room, he had his perspective back. His message to his happy players was that this was a moment for the fans; in real terms, it was just another three points. It would mean nothing if, at the end of the season, they failed to achieve enough points. In the end, the goals scored that day meant everything, as they provided the padding to City's goal difference, and the debit to United's, which would prove to be decisive in the final league table of the season.

That win came in October 2011 as City scorched to a record-breaking start to the season, but the planning had started in the hours after the FA Cup win in May, when Mancini had instantly turned his thoughts to the next target, winning the Premier League. With Tevez expected to move on, the top target was Atletico Madrid striker Sergio Aguero, while the Blues were also set to pursue Udinese winger Alexis Sanchez, Arsenal left back Gael Clichy and young Partizan Belgrade defender Stefan Savic.

By the time they reported back for pre-season training in early July, Clichy and Savic were in the bag, but Sanchez had opted to join Barcelona and the Blues had trained their sights on another Arsenal player, Samir Nasri, also wanted by neighbours United. City sold Jerome Boateng to Bayern Munich for £10 million, and shifted Jo from the payroll, while moves were afoot to finally clear out Bellamy as well. Not only that, City's owners had cooked up a £325 million sponsorship deal from Abu Dhabi's state-owned airline Etihad, which would ease the effects of Uefa's new financial fair play rules.

But Mancini made it plain he had been "disappointed" with the low speed at which City's transfer strategy was being conducted – he wanted deals done quickly so he could have a full pre-season with his entire squad. And he suggested that maybe the solution was for more power to be handed to the manager, so he would have a greater involvement in transfer and contract matters, and the appointment of medical staff. That harked back to the troubled days at Fiorentina, where Mancini had broken the Italian mould and become a general manager, with wide-ranging responsibilities and powers. He envied

Ferguson's role at United, which borders on all-powerful, within the financial constraints imposed by the owners. "He has been at United for a long time, so for him it is easy," said Mancini. "Maybe for me it's difficult because I have only been here for 18 months or so. Maybe I need to have more control of the team and the other situations . . . It's important for the manager to have control over the players and the medical staff and the other situations. It can improve. If the manager loses, the manager is sacked. Because of this I think the manager needs to take every decision and if he makes a mistake he pays for it."

With the deal for Aguero wrapped up and Nasri on the way, Mancini knew he finally had a squad which could challenge for the league title, and which could destroy the perception of his team as being too cautious, too negative. For half an hour in their opening fixture of the season, as newly-promoted Swansea City painted pretty patterns around their stodgy midfield, his optimism looked to be misplaced. But City rallied, and once Edin Dzeko had given City the lead, Aguero was brought on for his debut. He scored two more, the second a brilliant 30-yard dipping drive, to announce the arrival of a new Eastlands hero, and he also set up David Silva as they rattled up a 4–0 scoreline.

A 3–2 win at Bolton underlined City's attacking intent, but more significant was the trip to Tottenham the following week, which was billed as the first real test of the revamped Blues' title credentials. Harry Redknapp's side was simply blown away as Nasri made an impressive debut, Dzeko scored four and Aguero added another in a 5–1 win. United responded by hammering Arsenal 8–2 at Old Trafford – and it was plain this would be a very special year for Manchester football.

City got more reinforcements as they moved into September, with Owen Hargreaves joining the club on a free transfer after being released by United, while Kolo Touré had finished serving his ban for a positive drugs test. Aguero's hat-trick demolished Wigan, but the stunning league form did not carry over into the club's first Champions League tie. They appeared stage-struck against a lively counter-attacking Napoli side and only an Aleks Kolarov free kick rescued a point. Days later Aguero was back in the groove with two goals at Fulham, only for City to lose their way and drop their first league points of the season in a 2–2 draw.

They got straight back on track by beating bogey side Everton 2–0, with David Silva in sparkling form. Silva had been brilliant in the opening stages of the season, and Mancini – who usually prefers to extol team virtues rather than praise individuals – placed him in the highest bracket: "Silva is a top, top player. I don't know why he didn't go to Barca or Real Madrid, because he's Spanish, but we are lucky because he's here. If he had gone to Barca two years ago everyone would say he's one of the best players in the world – and he is one of the best players in the world. He's different from Messi and Cristiano Ronaldo because they are strikers and score a lot of goals, but I think he's the same as Xavi and Iniesta."

Any pretensions City might have had to be among the European elite as a team were blown away on a harrowing night in Munich, as Bayern inflicted their first defeat of the season, and gave them an object lesson in controlled, attacking football. The 2–0 result was overshadowed by the bust-up with Tevez, but Mancini backed his side to bounce back and still qualify from their group.

While the Tevez affair seized all the headlines, City simply carried on winning – and scoring. Four at Blackburn, four more against

Aston Villa sent City top, and a last-minute Aguero goal secured a first-ever Champions League victory over Villarreal. It had been the Blues' best start to a league season since 1897, and next up was the Manchester derby, with Mancini warning there could be no let-up if they were to hold on to top spot.

City fans were delighted with the way their team had begun the season, getting results and doing it with excellent football which had shut up the critics. After some doubt-filled moments in the last 18 months, Mancini had won over the fans, who sang his name loud – and doubled the volume as a show of support over the dispute with Tevez.

Heading for Old Trafford, there were still plenty of nerves, despite the feeling that their side was finally better than that of their Red rivals. City fans need not have worried. Balotelli scored twice, Aguero grabbed a third, and then sub Dzeko added a couple more, either side of Silva's well-deserved goal. The champions had been reduced to a rabble, over-run and outclassed in midfield and unable to cope with the pace and movement of Aguero and Balotelli, or the passing master-class of Silva.

The stunning victory was not just a watershed moment, but a complete vindication of Mancini's management style. Tevez was out in the cold, training alone, but displays of that magnitude do not come from teams which are riven by conflict and lacking in spirit and togetherness. The critics were eating their words, and Mancini was moving on to the next game, unmoved by the hype and euphoria, and thinking only of winning the title.

To emphasize their new strength in depth, Mancini then changed all 11 starting players for the Carling Cup tie at Wolves three days later – and the "second string" smashed in five goals, with Dzeko grabbing another brace. At the start of November, City had averaged 3.6 goals per league match, more than any other team in the top flight of any European league. Wolves were beaten again, this time in the league, despite the Blues being reduced to ten men by Vincent Kompany's red card. Then Villarreal were dispatched 3–0 on their own pitch, QPR were edged out 3–2 by Yaya Toure's header in a Bonfire Night thriller at Loftus Road, and Newcastle were seen off 3–1 at the Etihad in the clash of the two remaining unbeaten sides in the Premier League.

It had started to look as if the league "marathon" could turn into a canter for Mancini's splendid team, but his assistant David Platt said there was little chance of Mancini and his players falling for such hype: "There is a belief in them that they can do it and the manager is greedy, he wants everything. All he knows is winning and all he wants to do is win."

Adam Johnson was awarded a new five-year contract, a deal which came as a surprise to some as Mancini had been consistently reluctant to praise the young England winger. After he scored a goal and made another in the cup win at Wolves, the manager had found fault and been grudging in his praise. It could have been Aldo Mancini talking to his boy Roberto. Johnson found it exasperating, but there was a method in Mancini's meanness: "If he were not a good player, I wouldn't waste my time on him. But because he has everything, I don't want him stopping at this level," said Mancini.

Micah Richards had also been handed a new deal early in the season, just after his 23rd birthday, and he has also had the manager on his case to improve. "Micah is young," was Mancini's pronouncement. "In the last year he improved a lot as a player but I think he needs to improve more. He has good quality but sometimes

Micah is too strong and he thinks he can play at 50 per cent. If Micah plays to 100 per cent, for me he can become one of the top full backs in Europe."

The City fans were ecstatic at their team's start to the domestic season, but the Champions League was a different matter. City had been drawn in a particularly tough group, which featured four teams from the top four leagues in Europe. That was underlined as the Blues went to Napoli's intimidating Sao Paulo stadium and lost 2–1, with Edinson Cavani – who had scored at the Etihad in the first game between the two clubs – grabbing both goals. It was a sober "homecoming" for Mancini, whose wife and mother both hail from the region. It was also a reminder to the manager that, for all of his domestic successes with Inter, it was his failure in Europe which had ultimately cost him his job. To go through to the knockout phase, the Blues had to beat Bayern at home and hope that Napoli failed to win away to group whipping boys Villarreal.

Before that, there was a trip to Anfield on Mancini's 47th birthday, one of few grounds where victory still eluded him. It was not a particularly happy anniversary, even though Kompany scored from a corner to give the Blues the lead. Balotelli was harshly sent off and Charlie Adam's shot took a big deflection off Joleon Lescott for an equalizing goal.

Forty-eight hours later City faced a trip to Arsenal for a Carling Cup quarter-final, an oddity of the English fixture list which Mancini felt was damaging his team's chances of landing a trophy. As he prepared to make 11 changes, the manager said: "This is an incredible situation. Arsenal played on Saturday, we played Sunday evening and on Monday travel to London and then play Tuesday night. I think this is the reason why the national team arrive for

European Championships, World Cups and they are failing. The players don't have time to recover. To play again in two days like this so soon after the Champions League is incredible. We should play with 11 young players, maybe 14 or 15 years old, to make a statement."

At the Emirates both teams made ten changes and City went through to the semi-finals of the Carling Cup, thanks to a late goal by Sergio Aguero. Heading into December they maintained their five-point lead in the league, while United hung on to their coat-tails and hoped for a let-up in the pace as City sat on a record of 11 wins and two draws from their 13 league games. There was already talk of a lucrative new contract for the manager, but he made it plain that he wanted no distractions and would only begin negotiation once the season was finished.

He received strong backing from Sheikh Mansour, and a promise that he would be given time. In a rare interview the City owner said: "We are satisfied with the progress that is being achieved – the success and development at this level of football – but we must also continue to have patience. Sometimes I meet City supporters who criticize the work of the manager Roberto Mancini. In my opinion, his plans are on the right path. We need to reflect upon where the club has been and what we have achieved so far, and realize that what we have accomplished to date is formidable, but hard work is still required and it needs to be delivered with patience. We must not forget that our main objective is to win the English Premier League and if we achieve that, then it will have an impact on the team and the club as a whole and will show we can achieve anything."

The manager also got strong backing from the club over his handling of the Tevez affair, and the fact that his team was still going well at the top of the table showed that he had things under control. A 5-1 demolition of Norwich underlined that point, and as his side shaped up to face Bayern Munich, Mancini turned into a European statesman. He had shown himself to have little time for critics who knock City, preferring not to get into slanging matches and letting his team do the talking on the field. But when two powerful football figures turned their fire on the Blues ahead of the final round of Champions League games, the manager let loose with both barrels. Bayern supremo Karl-Heinz Rummenigge had been a constant critic of City – who had just posted record losses of £195 million – over their spending and the way they had conducted the transfer of Boateng. Now Rummenigge expressed a hope that they would be knocked out of the competition and suggested they should be thrown out of Europe if they did not meet the spending limits of Uefa's new financial fair play rules.

Mancini promised to seek out Rummenigge and ask him why he felt the need to constantly carp about his club, saying: "I think every team is worried about Manchester City because Manchester City in the future could become one of the top clubs in the world. But you don't want to see an important man like Rummenigge, who is the Bayern Munich chief executive and a representative of a top club in the world, saying things against us all the time. There are other teams in Europe that have a problem with financial fair play, not only Manchester City."

His vitriol was doubled when Napoli president Aurelio de Laurentiis made dark insinuations that there was something amiss as his team prepared to face Villarreal – he spoke of "strange things going on", as if City were somehow trying to influence the outcome of a game in which they needed the Italian side to slip up.

After all his experiences in Italy, as a victim of match-fixers and bent referees, Mancini was not impressed with his countryman: "Fortunately Sheikh Mansour is not Italian, because we are the teachers on what de Laurentiis said. Sheikh Mansour is not Italian and I don't think he is like this. De Laurentiis has to respect Villarreal firstly, because I think Villarreal is a serious club and when a team plays Champions League, they always play to win. And afterwards, show respect towards Sheikh Mansour because he doesn't know him, and Sheikh Mansour is a very good man. I can't think about this stupid situation."

De Laurentiis's words were proved to be nonsense as Napoli won in Spain and City's 2–0 victory over Bayern turned out to be meaningless. The Blues, along with United, were dumped into the Europa League, a competition which many fans perceived as a distraction from the task of winning the league. Mancini, who had won the Cup Winners' Cup with Sampdoria and Lazio as a player, knew that even the lesser European competition becomes a big thing once you get to the latter stages, and is also good experience for the Champions League.

There was no time for City to feel sorry for themselves. They had a hectic December and January schedule, and knew they would have to cope with the loss of midfield powerhouse Yaya Touré and defensive cover Kolo Touré for several games as the brothers headed off on African Nations Cup duty. Mancini vowed that if the Blues were still top by the time Yaya returned, they would take a lot of stopping in the charge for the Premier League finishing post. It was a bold pronouncement, and also spoke of how much the Blues relied on Yaya. With league games against Chelsea and Arsenal looming before Christmas, and an FA Cup third-round derby showdown with

United early in the new year, there would be little chance to
rest players.

Chelsea were the next big challenge, at Stamford Bridge, and
for 20 golden minutes it appeared another Old Trafford-style
annihilation might be on the cards. Balotelli and Aguero were
unplayable, and the former put City ahead early in the game. Silva
was denied a clear penalty as City dominated the game, and Chelsea
fans directed their ire at under-pressure manager André Villas-Boas.
But Chelsea hit back and after Raul Meireles had equalized and
Clichy had been sent off for two yellow cards, the Londoners won it
with a controversial Frank Lampard penalty. It was City's first league
defeat of the season, just 13 days before Christmas. Mancini was
unhappy about the non-award of the penalty, but told his players that
defeat makes you stronger, as long as you learn the lessons from it.

The lead over United was now down to two points, and in-form
Arsenal visited the Etihad Stadium with a record of seven wins
and a draw in their last eight games. With many pundits doubting
their title credentials, City narrowly won a classic encounter with a
scrappy Silva goal, and thanks to a brilliant display from goalkeeper
Joe Hart. The Blues then handed their fans the present of being
league leaders on Christmas Day as they dismissed Stoke 3–0, a result
which meant they had gone the entire calendar year of 2011 without
losing at home. Indeed, only Fulham and Napoli had managed draws
there, with City in fearsome mood on their home turf, racking up 26
wins from 28 games.

The Stoke game also marked the second anniversary of Mancini's
appointment, and the transformation in their fortunes was obvious.
But there were a few squally storm clouds gathering on the horizon,
not least Ivory Coast's refusal to bend on their insistence on having

the Touré brothers join their training camp a fortnight before the start of the Nations Cup – which meant they would miss the FA Cup tie with United and both legs of the Carling Cup semi-final against Liverpool, as well as vital league games.

Mancini was also not getting any benefit from players such as Emmanuel Adebayor, Roque Santa Cruz and Wayne Bridge, who were all draining wages from the club while out on loan – in Adebayor's case, scoring goals for title rivals Tottenham. In fact, with one eye on financial fair play, the club was increasingly insistent that the squad be trimmed of such excess. The size of the squad, and the juggling act to keep everyone happy, was causing problems. Adam Johnson had found it tough to get games since the arrival of Nasri in the summer, and he was concerned that not only was he becoming peripheral for City, he would also drift out of the mind of England manager Fabio Capello with the European Championships just six months away. He agreed with a rotation policy, he said, "as long as it's fair".

In key areas, however, notably central midfield and central defence, Mancini feared his squad was too light, and he was concerned that the need to sell might tie his hands for the second half of the season. Maybe that was behind his warning to his players and fans not to panic if they lost the top spot they had held since October 15: "I think we are strong enough to stay on the top, but we also know we can go into second position at some time. There are more than 20 games until the end." With 2011 still in its dying days, the manager, for the first time, dared to cast his eyes forward to April 30, and United's visit to the Etihad Stadium. "We know that if we want to win this league we need to play well to the end and beat them at home. If we are strong enough, I think it will be decided with that game at home, probably." That was quite a prediction, with another 17 league games to play before that derby, and many twists and turns to navigate.

Mancini was not happy that he was still short of a holding midfielder – the gamble on taking Owen Hargreaves on a year's contract had not paid off, with the former United man struggling for fitness. Now he would lose Yaya, who had just been named African Footballer of the Year, at a vital stage of the season with games coming thick and fast, and only Gareth Barry – who had been one of the players of the season to date – Nigel de Jong and James Milner to cover two positions. And when it came to Yaya's attacking abilities, there was no-one else with the same thrust and pace to change defence into attack.

Problems set in long before Yaya boarded the plane for Dubai, where the Ivory Coast were meeting ahead of their cup campaign. Indeed, he was in the team as City drew their first league blank of the season, a goalless draw at relegation-threatened West Bromwich Albion on Boxing Day. For once, the relentless Blue goal machine had malfunctioned, despite creating a multitude of chances. United romped to a 5–0 beating of Wigan, and the two Manchester clubs headed for the New Year holiday tied at the top on points, City clinging to the lead on goal difference. For the first time, the gleeful song of the City fans, declaring "We'll score when we want" had been silenced. A few days later, on New Year's Day in chilly Sunderland, it happened again. Korean striker Ji-dong Won was offside when he scored the Black Cats' last-minute winner, but Mancini directed his fire at his own players for their naïve defending. United had suffered a shock home defeat by bottom club Blackburn the day before, so City had spurned the chance to open a three-point lead.

The fixture switches for television had also put City at a disadvantage, as they faced Liverpool at home two days after the trip to Sunderland, which meant that the Merseysiders had two days of extra rest. The Blues passed the test, beating Kenny Dalglish's side 3–0, even though they lost Barry to a red card, to garner three welcome points with a horrendously tough January stretching ahead of them.

Going into the FA Cup third-round derby against United, the Blues had lost the Touré brothers to international duty, Barry to suspension, and Balotelli to injury. Ten minutes into the game they were also reduced to ten men when inspirational skipper Vincent Kompany was red-carded for a tackle which was two-footed but could hardly be described as dangerous or malicious. United forged into a 3–0 lead by half time, and City fans feared a reversal of their 6–1 win at Old Trafford three months earlier. Mancini's half-time switch was masterful, although it at first appeared to be damage limitation as attacking players Silva and Adam Johnson were replaced by defenders Savic and Pablo Zabaleta. But Mancini switched to three at the back, with Kolarov and Zabaleta working the flanks and Nasri and Aguero still providing an attacking threat. It worked brilliantly. United were rocked back, and goals from Kolarov and Aguero had the Reds clinging on against the ten men at the end. City were out of the cup, but the psychological boost of the comeback was to resonate through the rest of the season. Mancini would refer to it, with the title in the bag, as an important moment in their evolution as a team.

Kompany's red card, however, threw up another difficulty as it was his second of the season, bringing a four-match ban. Suddenly the absence of defender Kolo Touré became almost as big a deal as that of his younger brother Yaya. City considered recalling Dedryck Boyata from his season's loan at Bolton, and Mancini's complaints about a lack of players, ridiculed by some sections of the media, no longer looked as ludicrous as his critics painted them. The sense of injustice over Kompany was heightened three days after the FA Cup exit as the Blues lost the first leg of their Carling Cup semi-final at home to Liverpool. Stand-in defender Savic gave away the penalty which made the difference, and Glen Johnson escaped punishment for a two-footed tackle on Joleon Lescott which was much worse than the one which had seen Kompany handed such a stiff penalty.

Mancini afterwards expressed his indignation in a radio interview. Liverpool skipper Steven Gerrard overheard the interview and intervened, making out that the City boss was being hypocritical, as he had accused Wayne Rooney of trying to get Kompany sent off in the derby days earlier. Mancini said he had missed the point: "It was worse. It was clear it worse. I don't say this because I want Glen Johnson sent off, it was for the comparison. That tackle was worse than Vinny's."

Two defeats on the trot, and Mancini's increasing ire at perceived injustices, were touted as signs that the manager was cracking under the strain, something which he greeted with mirth as he recalled the intense pressures of managing Inter. Following their exit from one cup, and defeat at home in the semi-final first leg of another, the eyes of the football world were on the Blues as they headed to Wigan for a Monday night match. In a tight, tense match, Dzeko headed in the winner from a free kick and the Blues were again three points clear at the top. It had not been pretty, but Mancini implored his players to scrap their way through the next few weeks, until he got Kompany and the Touré brothers back.

Tottenham boss Harry Redknapp was next to try to ruffle Mancini, as his team and City prepared to do battle in a fight between first and third, with Spurs five points behind as they arrived at the Etihad. Redknapp intimated that anyone could win the title with the kind of financial backing Mancini had been given, and Mancini responded with a jokey suggestion that City might loan Spurs some cash. The game itself was another cracker, City taking a two-goal lead through Nasri and Lescott, but the visitors levelling through Jermain Defoe and a brilliant Gareth Bale strike. Defoe missed a great chance in stoppage time, but Balotelli earned and coolly converted a penalty to win the game 3–2, before being retrospectively banned for four games after TV slow-motion replays had revealed that he appeared to stamp on Scott Parker.

Three days later, the Blues could only draw in the second leg of the Carling Cup semi-final at Anfield. Again the referee, this time Phil Dowd, came under fire from Mancini as he awarded a penalty to Liverpool when Daniel Agger's shot bounced off Richards's leg and onto his arm. City were denied another clear spot kick of their own when Charlie Adam kicked the back of Dzeko's heel, and Mancini sardonically observed that the FA could punish Balotelli in hindsight but not correct the mistakes of Dowd by reviewing the video evidence. "I do feel a sense of injustice," he said. "In the last two months we have been very unlucky with referees. I haven't spoken to the referee – it's impossible to speak to him."

Six days later City were back on Merseyside and facing more problems, as another lack-lustre away performance saw them lose 1–0 to Everton, despite the return of Kompany from his ban. In the space of 23 days, City had gone out of both domestic cups, lost key players Kompany and Balotelli to four-match bans, and seen the

Touré brothers fly out on international duty. They were still clinging on to top spot, but they needed to snap out of their malaise quickly.

After talk of Italy international Daniele de Rossi as a possible shock transfer in the January window, City had to be content with 32-year-old loanee David Pizarro, who was out of the reckoning at Roma, but who had been a good player for Mancini at Inter. Keeper Costel Pantilimon's loan deal was also firmed up into a £3 million transfer from Timisoara.

They were not the only reinforcements – when the Blues submitted their new 25-man squad list for the Premier League at the end of the transfer window, it contained the name Carlos Tevez. With the window shut and nobody willing to pay the asking price, moves were afoot to bring the Argentine back into the fold.

A home clash with bad travellers Fulham, played out in a snowstorm, ushered in February. Aguero danced across the slippery surface with incredible poise and balance, Adam Johnson won a penalty and forced an own goal, and Dzeko benefited from a neat bit of generosity by Aguero late on for a comfortable 3–0 victory. When Lescott turned in the only goal at Aston Villa, Mancini's wish had been fulfilled – City were two points clear at the top as the Touré boys headed for home after Ivory Coast lost on penalties in the African Nations Cup final. And with Tevez finally saying he was sorry, and throwing himself into fitness training, there was a chance the Blues would be joined by another world-class striker just as the title race was getting interesting.

The Tourés met up with the squad in Portugal where City beat Porto in the first of two legs in the Europa Cup, and the following week the Blues confirmed their place in the last 16 with a crushing 4–0 win in the second leg.

With 13 league games to go, Mancini said every match was like a Champions League final. The lie was given to that statement when Blackburn and Bolton visited the Etihad in consecutive weeks, and were dispatched 3–0 and 2–0, Balotelli returning to action following his suspension to score a goal in each. All the while, Tevez was battling back to fitness, playing – and scoring – for the elite development squad, while Mancini praised his behaviour and application as "perfect" since he returned from his three-month self-imposed exile.

Things were going smoothly for City, traditionally a sign of impending disaster. United were matching the Blues win for win, to stay two points behind, but City were winning without playing well, the hallmark of champions. Then it came apart at the seams. A poor display in the Europa League tie at Sporting Lisbon, a 1–0 defeat, was bad enough, but Kompany limped off with a damaged calf 12 minutes in, and late in the game his replacement Lescott sustained a hip injury that would keep him out for nearly a month.

The Blues flew back from Portugal straight to south Wales for their game at Swansea, but their two first-choice centre backs headed back to Manchester for treatment. With Kolo Touré and Savic stepping in, the Blues were listless and dishevelled. They lost 1–0 as the young Montenegrin defender gave the ball away late in the game to gift the Swans a goal. United seized top spot for the first time in five months with a win over West Brom. At Swansea a TV camera caught one emotional City fan crying, but Mancini called for his players to have stouter hearts as they set about overhauling the Reds again.

A battling comeback from 2–0 down to win 3–2 in the second leg against Sporting brought a European exit which proved a blessing in disguise, as United crashed out to Athletic Bilbao on the same night. It was all or nothing for the two Manchester clubs – win the Premier League or finish the season empty-handed.

By the time they faced Chelsea at the Etihad, with Tevez named among the substitutes for the first time since that infamous night in Munich, City were four points adrift, with a game in hand. Mancini drafted Richards in as centre back, but the Blues went behind to Gary Cahill's goal with an hour played, and the title was starting to slip away. Mancini played his trump card, bringing on Tevez, and after Aguero had levelled from the penalty spot, his fellow Argentine produced a piece of magic to put Nasri in for the winner.

Fate appeared to intervene as top scorer Aguero was sidelined by a reaction to a painkilling spray which left his foot blistered. Mancini could barely hide his anger as he described the incident as "stupid" and demanded answers from his medical staff. Without Aguero the Blues were held to a 1–1 draw at Stoke, and their proud Premier League record run of 20 straight home wins ended in a 3–3 stalemate with Sunderland. The Blues were on the verge of losing to Martin O'Neill's side, trailing 3–1 with five minutes left, until Balotelli and Kolarov bagged goals which were ultimately to prove priceless. It was a draw which felt like a defeat at the time, but in the end it was a point snatched from the jaws of defeat, as United ploughed on relentlessly.

After the Stoke game Mancini made a pilgrimage to the holy church at Medjugorje in Bosnia, reputed to have been the scene of sightings of the Virgin Mary. Even the devout Mancini might have been moved to question his faith when, with Kompany and Lescott both back in harness, City went to Arsenal on Easter Sunday in a hopeful spirit. It went horribly wrong. With Balotelli hitting the self-destruct button, and the team performing poorly, they slid to a 1–0 defeat. United made it 11 wins from 12 with victory over Queen's Park Rangers, and it seemed the game was up. Coach David Platt would later reveal that no-one truly believed they had a chance of making up United's eight-point lead over the course of the last six games. But chairman Khaldoon al Mubarak headed for the dressing-room at the Emirates in a bid to lift spirits. He took Mancini to one side for a morale-raising chat which stuck with the manager. "We had two choices," Khaldoon later recalled. "We could either raise the white flag and sulk or pick ourselves up and fight until the last second of this championship. I remember going down to the dressing-room thinking we were not giving up. Something inside me said there was more to it. I had a conversation with Roberto. We both looked at each other and decided to take the pressure off everyone. We felt if we could win all our games and have a bit of luck, we could still pull it off. What Roberto did magnificently was to take the pressure off the entire team."

Manchester bookmaker Fred Done, a devout Red, was confident enough for Betfred to pay out on a United league win, and Mancini himself publicly declared that the race was over, while privately making sure his players were still fighting hard and would be ready if United did slip. The pressure was off City, and maybe United relaxed a little, too.

Three days after the shambles of the Emirates, and with the disgraced Balotelli suspended, Tevez made his first start since his return in the home game with West Brom, forming a rare partnership with Aguero. The Blues suddenly looked like the team that had hit the Premier League like a whirlwind in the first three months of the season. The Baggies were blitzed 4–0, with Tevez getting his first goal since his return from exile, and then news came through that United had surprisingly lost at Wigan, and the deficit was back down to five points.

Mancini was unmoved from his pronouncement that it was all over. On a personal level, his chat with Khaldoon had reassured him that he would keep his job as long as City did not implode in the run-in, even if the press was rife with speculation that he was being lined up for the chop. Privately, however, he felt there was now a whiff of a chance, and glum talk of the possibility of United winning the title at the Etihad, and the City players forming a guard of honour in front of their dejected fans, was pushed to the backs of minds.

City's superior goal difference had also been whittled down by their slump in form, and by United's surge in the run-up to Easter, and if the Blues could fight their way back into the race, they knew that could prove vital. So when they went to Carrow Road to play Norwich, a return to their free-scoring early-season ways was most welcome. Tevez hit a hat-trick and Aguero two as City proved unplayable in the latter stages of the match, running out 6–1 winners. Mancini stuck to his script, insisting the title race was "finished". United backed up his fatalistic words the following day with a 4–0 win over Aston Villa. But the Reds had got the message from the Blues' performance – the race was most definitely still on.

Mancini was already eyeing the following weekend's fixtures, when his team went to Wolves and United faced David Moyes's Everton, never an easy proposition, at Old Trafford. Mancini stirred the pot by suggesting that United were getting the benefit of helpful refereeing decisions after Ashley Young was given two dubious penalty decisions, while Tevez had been booked for diving at Norwich when he was clearly fouled in the box. As the City team coach made its way to Molineux from their team hotel, United led Everton 4–2 with seven minutes to go and the players were quiet. Then Nikola Jelavic and Steven Pienaar struck late in the game for an incredible 4–4 scoreline, and the City fans watching in Wolverhampton pubs, and the players hearing news on the coach, began to believe that something special was afoot.

They still had to win the game, with Wolves fighting for their Premier League lives, but a pass of quality from Clichy set up Aguero for the opener and Nasri added another in the second half. The equation was now simple – City could reclaim top spot by winning the derby the following Monday night. Mancini's view was predictable – even if the Blues won that game, he felt United would still win the title, as his team had to go to Newcastle in their penultimate game and the Reds had an easier finish to the season, playing Swansea and Sunderland.

Across the city, Ferguson was billing the game as "the derby of all derbies" – and so it proved, for City at least. There was little of the gorgeous, flowing football of which City were capable, but they put on a bloody-minded, determined, gutsy display. That was typified by the winning goal, skipper Kompany straining every sinew to rise above the defence and power home a header from a corner. Ferguson had put out a timid team which placed the emphasis on trying to stop City. That nervousness came out in their play, as they failed to have a shot on target in 90 minutes. It was too much for the United manager, as he picked an argument with Mancini, accusing him of "badgering" the officials. The City boss faced up to him in the technical area, and the City fans gleefully sang that "Fergie's cracking up". The Blues finally had a manager who would go toe to toe with the Red Baron, in football terms and in a good old-fashioned row, and that enhanced his growing legend in their eyes.

City were top again, and the fans were celebrating another derby triumph, but Mancini urged caution: "Newcastle will be our hardest game, harder than United," he said. "It is strange, but it is like this. They have had a fantastic season, are playing to get into the Champions League, and their manager is one of the best managers in England. It will be a tough game. We were happy for the crowd on Monday night but it is important our supporters do not think it is finished. We need to be very calm. We need to concentrate on the next game, work well, and recover. The message is to keep calm, like one and two weeks ago. Nothing has changed."

Silva confirmed that Mancini's ploy of insisting the title race was over had taken the pressure off the team and given them the freedom to play their way back into contention. Now the heat was back on as City headed for Newcastle, who were fighting for a possible Champions League spot. The tension was raw and unrelieved for 70 minutes, and then Yaya Touré picked the moment to show his world class. An almost nonchalant swing of the right boot sent the ball curving beyond keeper Tim Krul, and in the final minute he flipped in a close-range second to secure a remarkable 2–0 win.

Behind the scenes in the stadium, City officials were hugging and high-fiving, but Mancini did not join in with any of the euphoria. With one more win needed to seal the title, the most he would admit was that his team had "two fingers" on the title.

His minimal optimism was misplaced, surely. That victory had to be gained over lowly Queen's Park Rangers, at fortress Etihad, backed by a fervent packed house. Mancini was on the cusp of everlasting Blue glory. It would all be so straightforward and decisive … wouldn't it?

Index

Index

Index

Index

Index

Index

Picture Credits

The publishers would like to thank the following sources for their kind permission to reproduce the pictures in this book.